ALEA JACTA EST !

GOSCINNY AND UDERZO
PRESENT
AN ASTERIX GAME BOOK

THE ROMAN
CONSPIRACY

TRANSLATED BY ANTHEA BELL AND DEREK HOCKRIDGE

HODDER AND STOUGHTON
LONDON SYDNEY AUCKLAND TORONTO

British Library Cataloguing in Publication Data

Uderzo
The Roman conspiracy.
1. French humorous strip cartoons
I. Title   II. Goscinny, *1926-1977*   III. Series
IV. L'affaire des faux menhirs
741.5944

ISBN 0-340-51423-X

Published by Hodder and Stoughton Children's Books,
a division of Hodder and Stoughton Ltd,
Mill Road, Dunton Green, Sevenoaks, Kent TN13 2YA

Typeset by SX Composing, Rayleigh, Essex

Printed in Belgium by Proost International Book Production

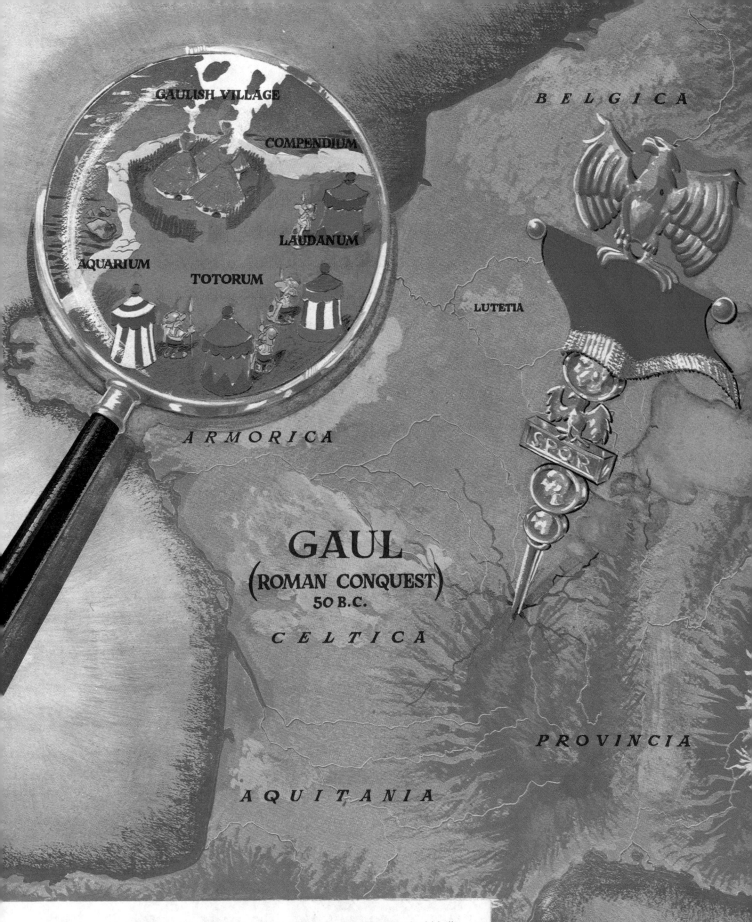

GAUL
(ROMAN CONQUEST)
50 B.C.

BELGICA

LUTETIA

ARMORICA

CELTICA

AQUITANIA

PROVINCIA

GAULISH VILLAGE

COMPENDIUM

LAUDANUM

AQUARIUM

TOTORUM

The year is 50 BC. Gaul is entirely occupied by the Romans. Well, not entirely . . . One small village of indomitable Gauls still holds out against the invaders. And life is not easy for the Roman legionaries who garrison the fortified camps of Totorum, Aquarium, Laudanum and Compendium . . .

ALEA JACTA EST!

HERE IS A NEW KIND OF ASTERIX BOOK...

YOU ARE JUSTFORKIX, THE HERO OF THIS STORY. YES, YOU YOURSELF ARE JUSTFORKIX, A YOUNG MAN FROM LUTETIA. WE KNOW SOMETHING ABOUT YOU ALREADY, FROM 'ASTERIX AND THE NORMANS'. IN THAT BOOK, YOUR FATHER SENT YOU TO THE LITTLE GAULISH VILLAGE TO TOUGHEN YOU UP A BIT. MAYBE YOU DON'T HAVE QUITE THE STRENGTH OF OBELIX, OR THE WISDOM OF GETAFIX, OR EVEN THE EXPERIENCE OF ASTERIX, BUT NOBODY'S PERFECT...

AND YOU ARE NOW ABOUT TO FACE DREADFUL DANGERS. FROM PARAGRAPH TO PARAGRAPH, FROM PERIL TO PERIL, YOU WILL HAVE TO MAKE DIFFICULT DECISIONS, TAKE RISKY ACTION, THROW THE DICE AND SEE WHAT LUCK CHANCE BRINGS YOU, GET YOURSELF OUT OF COMPLICATED SITUATIONS, SOLVE KNOTTY PROBLEMS. YOU WON'T ALWAYS BE SUCCESSFUL... AND IF YOU AREN'T, YOU WILL HAVE TO BEGIN THE ADVENTURE AGAIN.

BUT NEVER DESPAIR! REMEMBER THAT YOU ARE AN INDOMITABLE GAUL...

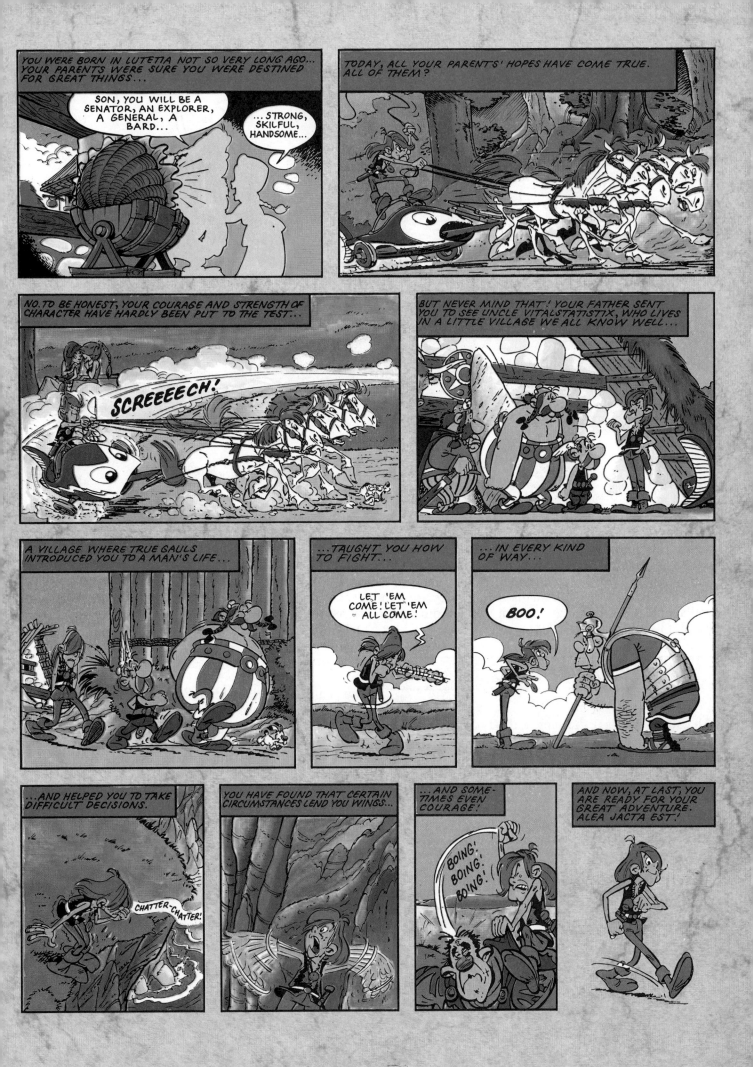

RULES OF THE GAME

You are going to have a thrilling and dangerous adventure in this book; you can be sure of that! But you may not be quite so sure how to play it yet.

So read the following rules carefully. They apply to all the ASTERIX game books in this series. They are clear and simple – don't hesitate to turn to them during the game if necessary.

CHANCE BOARD

All you need to play the game is this book, a pencil, and an eraser so that you can rub pencil marks out and play the game again. If you happen to have a dice, that's fine. But don't worry if you haven't. You can use the Chance Board which you will find at the end of the book.

ADVENTURE SLAB

You take the Adventure Slab with you on your adventures. It will come in useful when you want to note something down as a reminder, leaving you free to put your mind to other problems. You can detach it from the rest of the book, and then you get two for the price of one.

PERSONAL QUALITIES

Take a look at your Adventure Slab. You start out with three personal qualities.
- *Skill.*
- *Fighting Fitness.*
- *Charm.*

Each quality carries a number of points. It's up to you to decide on your own personality knowing that:
– you already have 10 points for each quality,
– you have an extra 15 points to divide between your qualities at the beginning of the adventure.

Record your choice on the Adventure Slab. Adding up the number of points your three qualities carry, you should get 45. If you don't get 45, either you've made a mistake or you've been cheating already!

SECONDARY APTITUDES

Needless to say, you weren't born yesterday, and you've already knocked about Gaul a bit. So you've learned some useful little tricks to use from day to day. At the beginning of the adventure, and sometimes in the middle of it, you will be told to choose between various aptitudes. Select whichever seems to you most useful, and remember to write it down on your Adventure Slab.

OBJECTS

A good legionary never goes anywhere without equipment. You can choose various objects which may turn out useful during your adventure, though on the other hand they may be more of a nuisance than anything else. And you can take only 5 objects. If you come across some other object during your travels and you want to take it with you, but you already have 5, you must get rid of one of them. You will find out what objects you can take in one of the early chapters.

NB: the gourd of magic potion and the purse of sestertii do not count as objects. They are extra items of equipment.

FIGHTS

Knowing you, you're bound to find yourself in situations where a punch-up or a spot of sword-play is called for.

To find out the result of your fights, follow these rules:

1. Enter your Fighting Fitness points in one of the Fights spaces on your Adventure Slab, plus any points that certain objects earn you – for instance, a sword or a shield.

2. Now write down your enemy's points. (You will find these given in the text.)

3. Throw the dice, or use the Chance Board, and subtract the number you get from your enemy's points score.

4. Throw the dice again, and subtract the number you get from your own score.

5. Carry on in the same way until your score or your enemy's score reaches 0. The loser is whichever of you reaches 0 first.

6. Unless there is any instruction telling you otherwise, you start again with the same original number of points next time you fight.

Example: a centurion takes you by surprise and challenges you to a duel. Suppose your score for Fighting Fitness is 15 and the centurion's score is 12. If you also have a sword (+5) and a shield (+3), your actual score for Fighting Fitness is thus 15+5+3 = 23.

Well done! You have won this particular fight . . . but it might not always be so easy.

NB: your Skill or Charm may also be used in a fight, depending on circumstances. When the time to use them comes, of course, you will be told.

FIGHTS AGAINST MORE THAN ONE ENEMY

In fights of this kind, you will be told either your enemies' total Fighting Fitness, and you have only one fight, or their individual Fighting Fitness, and you have more than one fight on your hands. But a word of warning . . . when fighting two enemies separately, and only then, you do not get your original Fighting Fitness score back to fight the second; you start with whatever points you have left from the first of the two fights.

TESTS

In certain other circumstances you may not have to fight an enemy, but you still have to pass a test of Skill, Fighting Fitness or Charm, using those qualities to get yourself out of a tricky situation. When that happens, follow these rules:

1. Always write down your points score for whichever quality is concerned, plus any extra points certain objects give you.

2. The degree of difficulty will always be given for each test, for instance: *difficulty 4*.

3. Now throw the dice as many times as the degree of difficulty indicates, for instance: *difficulty 4 = 4 throws* of the dice, *difficulty 5 = 5 throws*.

4. Each time you throw the dice, subtract the number you get from your own points score.

5. If you are left with a number above 0, you have succeeded. If you get 0 or a minus number, you have failed.

6. Unless you are told otherwise, you start again with your original points score when the next test comes up.

Example: you have to pass a test of skill with a difficulty factor of 4. You start with 14 points for Skill. You throw the dice 4 times and subtract the number from 14; for instance, $14 - 3 - 5 - 1 - 3 = 2$. As the result is above 0, you have succeeded.

MAGIC POTION

If you drink some of Getafix's magic potion, you automatically win a fight or succeed in a test of your Fighting Fitness without needing to follow the usual rules. When the fight or the test is over, you lose your superhuman strength. You will then have to face the next fight or test in the usual way, unless you drink another dose of magic

potion. Your gourd holds five doses at the beginning of your adventure.

Remember that:

– The magic potion will not work in fights or tests which call for you to use your personal qualities of Skill or Charm.

– You can drink magic potion only at the beginning of a fight or a test, never in the middle of it.

Keep a record of the number of doses of potion left in your gourd on your Adventure Slab.

PURSE

You are sure to need money on your travels. You must keep careful note of the number of sestertii you spend on your Adventure Slab.

THE END OF THE ADVENTURE

Sometimes, when you have lost a fight or made an error of judgment, you will read the fateful words: 'YOUR ADVENTURE IS OVER'.

Then you must start again at Chapter I.

CHAPTER I

THE MORNING AFTER THE NIGHT BEFORE

A student's lot is quite a happy one – and a lot (of money) is what you need to enjoy all the fun of Lutetia properly. How did you earn it? Reciting poetry in taverns, running in your friends' new chariots, or selling Lux Solis* soap door-to-door? *Choose one answer and enter this secondary aptitude (poetry, chariot-running-in, selling soap) on your Adventure Slab.* How nice to spend your hard-earned sestertii! This evening, for instance, you've been to the Vandal's Arms to listen to the Genesix group, currently Number I in the Top XX. After the gig the innkeeper stood barley beer all round and there was some pretty wild dancing . . . you were glad to get to bed after such a memorable evening. But you'll be right as rain when you've slept it off.

* Sunlight

● Go to 1.

'Justforkix! JUSTFORKIX!!!' The voice of your father Doublehelix rudely awakens you after your night out on the town with beer and old Rolling Menhirs* songs. He is shaking you with all his (considerable) might.

'Look at this slab from my brother Vitalstatistix! His village is having a barley beer festival and you're invited. You lucky lad! And see, there's a postscript carved by Cacofonix, asking you to bring the latest odes by Genesix for the villagers to enjoy. Well, what do you say?'

- Poor Doublehelix! The only reply he gets is a loud snore. Go to **33**.
- You bravely get up, tired as you feel, saying, 'Good idea! I'll leave as soon as possible.' Go to **5**.
- You grumble, 'Huh! I'd rather go into town. I'm seeing my friend Surprisepartix tomorrow, and we'll probably have a Hades** of a time.' Go to **7**.

* See ASTERIX AND THE NORMANS.

** Roman Hell

2

The landlord flies off the handle. 'What? Moon about here tasting my barley beer for two months? Are you trying to be funny, by Toutatis?'

To make matters worse, while he is bawling you out a

Roman patrol hears the racket and comes to investigate. The centurion decides that in present circumstances Gauls must be treated firmly.
- Escorted by six legionaries, you go off to **30**.

3

Walking is so tiring! No sooner are you out of sight of Lutetia than weariness overcomes you. If only a chariot would stop and give you a lift! *Take a test of Charm (difficulty 4) to see if any charioteer likes the look of you.*
- If you succeed, climb in and go to **18**.
- If you fail, go and kick your heels at **40**.

4

The escort takes you straight to a dungeon in the palace of the Consul of Lutetia, Longtoreignoverus. It is dark and the straw is damp, but you have company: there is a shape in one corner, apparently asleep. Only when day dawns are you amazed to recognise . . . your father Doublehelix, chained up beside you. He tells you his sad story.

'I was just off to deliver a few menhirs for Obelix when some Roman soldiers turned up. Their centurion yelled, "That's him! Arrest him!" It was all so sudden I couldn't get away. I was taken before the Consul of Lutetia, who said I was under arrest for selling counterfeit menhirs. Of course I protested my innocence, but it was no good. They threw me into this dungeon.'

Doublehelix is interrupted by the sound of footsteps. A key turns in the lock . . .

- You must flee. Go to **38**.
- You are both innocent. Surely the Consul will realise that it was an unfortunate judicial error. This is probably the Consul coming in now, at **31**.

5

Doublehelix looks delighted.

'Good idea, son! A few months by the seaside will do you good.'

'Wait a minute,' you say. 'My chariot has a broken axle, and I took it in to Chariotmechanix down at the garage. How am I going to get to Armorica?'

11

'Easy! My old friend Intercitix drives a public cart on the Lutetia-Totorum-Laudanum-Aquarium-Compendium route. And the way those garrisons chop and change all the time, you can bet he has a very busy time! If I ask him, he'll drop you off quietly near Asterix and Obelix's village.'
● Your bundle is soon packed, and you're ready to leave from **9**, taking the latest odes by Genesix, *which you enter as an object on your Adventure Slab.*

● You fancy seeing a play. You decide to go to the amphitheatre where Ovid is packing them in, at **39**.
● You make for the Latin Quarter. You're sure to find some friends there. Go to **21**.

8

'Come in, Justforkix. I'm glad you've come to see us.'
Getafix seems worried. 'I have a feeling someone has designs on Obelix's menhirs,' he goes on. 'And I'm wondering why. There could be some kind of conspiracy here.' He stops for a moment, doubtfully. Then he looks at you with a slight smile. 'I want you to find out what's up. You can pass incognito more easily than Asterix and Obelix. But be careful. This could be dangerous!'
● Trembling slightly, you stammer, 'I . . . I'll have to think it over.' Go back to the village gates.

6

A legionary's voice is heard at the exit. 'Checking all slablets! This way, please! Show your entry slablets! Hurry up now, please!'
Bother! The only way to avoid serious trouble is to get lost in the crowd . . . *Take a test of Skill (difficulty 3) to escape the Romans.*
● If you fail, the furious centurion takes you off to **30**.
● If you succeed, hurry home to **33**.

7

There's plenty of entertainment in Lutetia. Much better than a village festival.

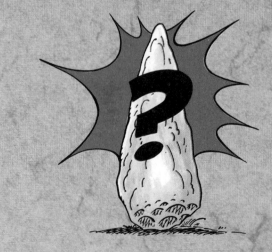

● Puffing out your chest, you announce proudly that you would never let your friends down, Gaul expects that every man will do his duty, etc. (can't even stop to think before opening your big mouth, can you?). Go to **46**.

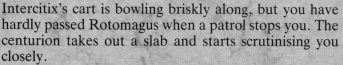

9

Intercitix's cart is bowling briskly along, but you have hardly passed Rotomagus when a patrol stops you. The centurion takes out a slab and starts scrutinising you closely.

- You wait patiently until he's through. Go to **13**.
- You launch straight into an explanation. Go to **15**.
- You whisper to Intercitix, 'Here goes!' Go to **35**.
- Jumping down, you try to seize the centurion's sword. Go to **44**.

10

The voice replies, 'We've come to search Doublehelix's house, by order of the Consul!'
- There's no time to lose. You slip out through the back door. Go to **20**.
- You shout through the door, 'Why does the Consul want to search the house?' Go to **41**.

11

You may know where to go and whom to see.
- If you do, set off for **37**, with one last look back at the village. You won't be seeing it for some time.
- If not, get as many advantages as possible on your side before taking a decision. Go back to the village.

12

They haul you straight on board! You're being taken for a ride – in the consular militia's Maria nigra.
- A swift drive through the streets of Lutetia, and you reach **4**.

13

'No doubt about it, that's him! Oh, won't the Consul be pleased when he hears we've captured Doublehelix's son!'

By Toutatis, you seem to be in trouble. What does all this mean? You're making for Lutetia chained up in a Roman chariot. After a day's driving, the smoke of the great Gallo-Roman city appears in the distance.
- The future looks as dark as the Consul's prison, and that's saying a lot. Go to **4**.

14

'Ah, Justforkix! Here you are at last! A real music-lover is always welcome out in the Styx* here. I haven't had a chance to perform in public since your last visit, but I've been hard at work, and I have a little surprise for you – a collection of my best compositions.' *You can enter it on your Adventure Slab.* 'Have you brought me the latest odes by Genesix?' *Look at your Adventure Slab.*
- Yes . . . Go to **42**.

• No . . . The bard is slightly disappointed. 'Oh well, never mind, it's a pleasure to see you anyway. As soon as you have a spare moment I'll play you one of my latest works.' You don't feel like facing the music yet, so you take a little walk round the village.

* Roman river of death

15

'We're not brigands, we're harmless travellers. I'm going to visit my family. They live far away in Armorica, and they haven't seen me for ages. I'm sure you wouldn't want to delay a nephew's reunion with . . .'

Will the centurion be deceived by your smooth talk? *Take a test of Charm (difficulty 4). Yes, difficulty 4, because this centurion fought at Alesia, and it's hard to convince a tough nut like him.*
• You convinced him? He lets you go on your way to **22**, even wiping away a tear with the end of his pilum.
• Oh, help! It didn't work? The centurion saw through your patter. Go to **13**.

16

Getting in without paying may not be very honest, but it's easy. Getting out again is trickier. *Throw the dice.*
• *If you throw 1, 2 or 3,* go to **6**.
• *If you throw 4, 5 or 6,* go and have a rest at **33**. It's midnight already, and you need some sleep.

'I think Vitalstatistix can tell you more than I can.' Asterix seems worried, and for once he's not being very talkative.

• If you have already been to see Vitalstatistix, go and visit someone else.
• If not, go and knock on his door at **24**.

18

By Belisama, what irresistible charm you have!
• Rustix, driving his ox-cart, stopped at once and drove you to the village gates at **22**.

19

The door is wide open. One bound and you are out in the corridor, which is deserted at this time of day. The great hall of the consul's palace is crammed with Gauls. You can just stroll out. Free again! But now what? Do you go home or do you hide?

- The road home leads to **26**.
- There's still one possible hiding place; the village where your Uncle Vitalstatistix lives, but you must resign yourself to walking there, since you have just remembered that your chariot is in at Chariotmechanix's garage for repair. Walk to **3**.

20

The back yard is full of returned amphoras. You have to get through them without making any noise. To do so, *take a test of Skill (difficulty 3)*.
- If you fail, the centurion discovers your ruse and catches up with you at **12**.
- If you succeed, you find yourself in the next street, and you have time to lose yourself in the crowd. Phew! A little relaxation wouldn't come amiss. Go to **7**.

21

After a few hours in an Arvernian tavern, your boredom and anxiety give way to pleasant dreams . . .
    'YOUR BILL, SIR!!!'

The return to reality is harsh: Nothingontix the landlord is holding a slab covered with figures under your nose.
- Your purse is full of sestertii, and you settle the bill easily. Go to **43**.

- You must bargain. *Take a test of Charm (difficulty 5)*. Every sestertius counts. If you sound convincing, the landlord agrees to give you credit, but you'd better not hang around. Go to the amphitheatre at **39**. If you don't succeed in mollifying him, go to **2**.
- 'I'll pay by washing dishes,' you tell him. This seems to suit the landlord, who points in the direction of the kitchens. Go to **29**.

22

The village at last! Who are you going to visit?
- *To choose your destination, look at the right-hand page and use the numbers of the paragraphs indicated on the picture of the village. You can move about freely.*

23

'I hope Genesix isn't one of those heavy metal bands. I'm no slouch in that line myself, so watch out!'
    Fulliautomatix is leaning on the hammer Cacofonix knows so well. You try to calm him down.
    'No, no, they're only a group of bards who declaim odes in the catacombs.' (You liar!) 'Don't worry, you can't hear a thing from here.'
    'Good.'
    He even smiles briefly and turns to his forge, where you hear him rummaging among his tools. He comes out carrying a small anvil.

'Here, this is for you. I'm sure you don't get enough healthy exercise in the big city.' *But if you want to take the anvil it counts as 3 objects.*
• Make your choice and continue your round of visits.

24

Your Uncle Vitalstatistix looks preoccupied. When you question him, he explains.

'It's like this, lad. The village was getting cluttered up with Obelix's menhirs. So Getafix and I had the idea of exporting them to the rest of Gaul. We brought Doublehelix in on the deal as he supplies Gaulish souvenirs to the big Selfrix's store. So far we've been very successful, but I've just heard from Postaldistrix the postman that Doublehelix has been arrested by order of the Consul. It seems he's accused of trafficking in counterfeit menhirs. We don't have much time to get him out of trouble because the Consul has declared that the culprits will set off to row in Caesar's galleys on the Ides of March.'

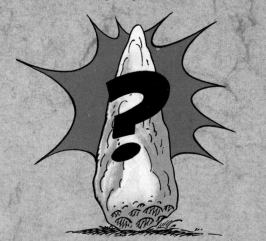

Of course, you offer your help. Vitalstatistix gladly accepts although at first he doesn't know just what mission to give you.

'But anyway, take this,' he says, handing you a sword. *Add it to your Adventure Slab if you decide to take it. The sword gives you a bonus of 5 extra Fighting Fitness points.*
• Now, where will you go next? Take a look at the picture of the village.

25

A moaning menhir – whoever heard of such a thing? However, on approaching you hear two very familiar voices.

'Don't cry like that, Obelix. There must be some mistake.'

'Oh, by Toutatis! My lovely, lovely menhirs!'
'I'm sure we'll find some solution. Hello there – it's Justforkix! What a surprise!'
Asterix interrupts his conversation with his best friend to greet you.
• You want to know more, so you ask Asterix. Go to **17**.
• You don't like to interfere, so you just ask for the latest village news. Go to **36**.

26

'Hello, young fellow! Going far?'
A shiver runs down your spine, and you turn round, trembling, to see . . . good old Intercitix who drives the public cart.
'I'm afraid I can't hang around,' he goes on, 'because I'm off to your Armorican friends to deliver some barrels of barley beer. If you'd like a chat, why not come along?'
Not a bad idea. The air of Lutetia doesn't suit you too well just now.
• You get into Intercitix's cart and go to **9**.

27

Unfortunately for you, the Romans were legion, and a legion intent on coming in. They break the door down. You might be said to be in an awkward position. Bad luck, because YOUR ADVENTURE IS OVER.

28

'Why, if it isn't Justforkix! I hope you haven't come to encourage Cacofonix. He keeps talking about something called Genesix. Do you know this Genesix?'

● You cautiously pretend you don't. You ask after his constitution (of iron) and his nerves (of steel) and realise that his musical tastes haven't changed. You go back to the village square.
● 'Yes, of course I know Genesix,' you reply. Go and continue the conversation at **23**.

29

Your bill comes to 78 sestertii, and in a week of dishwashing you will pay off one as*. Do the sum (you'll be washing a lot of dishes) . . . but why bother? YOUR ADVENTURE IS OVER.

*One sestertius = two and a half asses

30

The legionaries taking you away strike up an old Latin Quarter song: 'It was Saturnalia Day in the cookhouse . . . ' You feel your troubles are only just beginning. When you come in sight of the Consul's palace, you overhear a remark of the centurion's.
'Well done, lads. We've picked up Doublehelix's son!'
● Go to **4**. This is a really bad start!

31

'Soup's up!'
The footsteps were those of a jailer bringing your food: stewed fabae*. He adds, nastily, 'Better eat it slowly. This will be the only meal you'll get for the whole week.'
As an investigator, you're a has-bean. YOUR ADVENTURE IS OVER.

*Broad beans

32

'You've come at a good time, Justforkix. I've just had a delivery of nice fresh tructae*.'
From the smell of them, you suspect they must have come all the way from Rome on slave-back, but you

don't want to hurt his feelings. You pretend to be so interested that he offers you a fish. If you accept, *enter it on your Adventure Slab*, but nobody's forcing you . . .
● All things considered, you decide to continue your walk round the village.
*Trout

33

In peace and quiet at last, you sleep the sleep of the just. But this is not your lucky day. A violent knocking at the door suddenly wakes you from your dreams. This is too much! Infuriated, you make for the doorway, determined to send whoever it is away with a flea in his ear. Just as you reach the door, you are startled to hear the words: 'Open up in the name of the Consul!'

● You don't want to advertise your presence, so you slip out of the back door. Go to **20**.
● You question the Roman through the door, trying to find out what he wants. Go to **10**.
● You shout, 'This residence is Gaulish, and Gaulish it will stay! You come in only over my dead body!' Reap the reward of your courage (or your recklessness) at **27**.

34

The centurion produces a slab from his tunic and inspects you carefully. *Convincing him that you were only passing through is a test of Charm (difficulty 4).*
● If you succeed, go to recover from your fright at **7**.
● If you fail, the centurion, now sure that you were trying to trick him, grabs your collar. Go to **12**.

35

By Toutatis! It's just like 'The Charge of the Light Cohort'. You heard the poet Tennysonius recite his famous work in the arena only last week. It's a violent business, but you have a chance of escaping. The patrol consists of four legionaries and a centurion.

First you need to know which enemies you are escaping. Throw the dice for each of them. If you do not throw the number written underneath the legionary in question, you have got away from your enemy. If you escape him, cross him out; if not, you must fight. When you have finished, add up the Fighting Fitness of the enemies you failed to escape, and fight them all at once (the legionaries are young recruits without much training or Fighting Fitness; however, their centurion is a beefy character with a Fighting Fitness score of 15).
● If you beat them, Intercitix takes you to **22**.
● If not, go to **13**.

36

Obviously Asterix isn't really happy about replying.
'Justforkix, you know what a quiet life we lead here. Nothing of any interest to a Lutetian goes on in

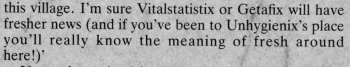

this village. I'm sure Vitalstatistix or Getafix will have fresher news (and if you've been to Unhygienix's place you'll really know the meaning of fresh around here!)'

• If you haven't visited them already, now's your chance.
• If you have, stroll around the village.

37

Hang on, haven't you forgotten something? Stop and think . . . you turn straight back.

'Uncle Vitalstatistix! How to do you expect me to get by on the roads of Gaul without any money?'

'By Belenos, you're right! I'm woolgathering!'

Vitalstatistix gets a Roman helmet down from a shelf and produces a handful of sestertii. *Throw the dice and refer to the table below to see how much money you start out with. Write the amount on your Adventure Slab.*

YOUR DICE	I	II	III	IV	V	VI
YOUR SESTERTII	30	35	45	54	75	99

• Pockets full, you leave your uncle and set out on your adventure at **47**.

38

WHAM! A mighty kick overturns the bowlful of fabae* the jailer has just brought you for your meal. Can you manage to bean him with your usual skill and accuracy? *Take a test of Skill (difficulty 3).*

• If you miss, go to **45**.
• If you hit the target, well done! You should be in the Olympics. But meanwhile, go to **19**.
*Broad beans

39

What a crowd! Magnificent tunics and togas pass before your dazzled eyes. Unfortunately, you are short of asses*, and as there is to be only one performance you must choose between:
• Going in without paying. Go to **16**.
• Drinking to drown your disappointment, if you haven't already met Nothingontix. Go to **21**.
• Going home to bed, because after all, a good night's sleep would do you good. Go to **33**.
*Units of Roman coinage

40

Too worn out to go back, too tired to go on, you surrender to the first Roman soldier you meet. Obviously you aren't a real Gaulish warrior yet. YOUR ADVENTURE IS OVER.

41

Under the united efforts of the Roman soldiers the door eventually falls in. The centurion commanding them grabs you.

'You're very inquisitive, aren't you, young man? Are you by any chance related to Doublehelix?'

You reply:
- 'Yes, I'm his son.' This cheers the centurion up no end. Go to **12**.
- 'No, I only came to visit his son.' The centurion frowns. Go to **34**.

42

'How glad I am that you thought of me! I promise that you shall have the very best seats when I sing in a real gala performance. Meanwhile, would you please accept these small gifts?'

Suiting the action to the word, Cacofonix gives you a lyre (obviously second-hand) and a papyrus, making it clear that they are presents. *Don't forget to enter them on your Adventure Slab*.
- Continue going round the village.

43

Where did all that money come from? Unless you can prove otherwise, you haven't had a chance to get hold of any yet. Justforkix, you're cheating!
- Hurry back to **21** and find an honest solution.

44

This manoeuvre has surprised the centurion. He tries to draw his sword before you reach him. *Take a test of Fighting Fitness (difficulty 4)*.
- You succeed, and carry on full speed ahead to **22**.
- You fail! You'll be had up for assault, and your prospects don't look good. Go to **13**.

45

You're not so full of fabae* now. The jailer will be on his guard, and he isn't about to let you go. YOUR ADVENTURE IS OVER.

*Beans

46

'Justforkix, my boy, we need your help. Here is something very valuable to help you in a tight spot; a gourd of magic potion, containing two doses.' *Put it on your Slab*.

Getafix continues. 'You must go to Rome. That's where all the action is. Go and see my friend Spurius Virus the doctor. He'll be happy to give you aid and assistance. And don't forget to keep your eyes open, because you'll be making some careful enquiries.' *Don't hesitate to note down any clues you may gather on your Adventure Slab*. They will come in useful for discovering the key to the mystery of a crime never before known in Rome; trafficking in counterfeit menhirs.
- If you haven't been to see Vitalstatistix yet, do so at once, before your uncle takes offence. Go to **24**.
- If you have, the whole village is open to you, and you can choose where you go.

CHAPTER II

MAKE YOURSELF AT HOME

47

It's a long journey. Getafix advised you to stop for a night at an inn near Lugdunum, famous for its good inns and hotels. He also gave you a Michelix slab. After consulting it, you decide to stay at:
- Bocus. Go to **53**.
- Trusthousefortix. Go to **61**.
- The Anorexix Inn. Go to **75**.

48

You can see columns in the background. That must be a peristyle, and you can hear snatches of conversation.
- Go to **78**.
- Or open the door at **128**.
- Or if you have found what you were looking for, leave the villa at **145**.

49

You obviously know animal language. Bulimix (the dog's name, for obvious reasons) throws himself on the food. The way is clear. Take your chance and go in.
- Go to **74**.

50

Wheelerdealus really is resourceful. He must be a big wheel among shopkeepers. If you buy something, *enter it on your slab* – and don't forget to pay. Wheelerdealus gives you a bag for your provisions, and *everything you buy from him counts as a single object in all*.
- Your purchases made, go back to **77**.

51

'Fish? Let's have a look.'

You take the fish you brought from the village out of your bag. Wheelerdealus flinches.

'What a stink!' he cries. 'By Jupiter, that must be a very unusual speciality. I never smelt anything like it before. There'll be plenty of rich people anxious to buy something so unusual. I'll give you 150 sestertii for it.'

An old village saying comes to mind as you pocket the 150 sestertii. These Romans are crazy! *Take the fish off your list of objects.*

● Go to **77**.

52

'Phew! What an unsavoury dish! How do you make it?'

'It's one of the specialities of the house, made with Armorican fish. Our supplier had an extra-fresh delivery this morning. Maybe you know him. The name's Wheelerdealus.'

You certainly do! You also know where that fish came from. This affair could kick up quite a stink! But it's time to take your researches more seriously. Your delicate stomach won't get over this in a hurry. *Subtract 1 point of Fighting Fitness while you are in the villa.*

● Go back to **78**.

53

You can easily identify Bocus's restaurant from the number of foreign chariots parked outside and the subtle aromas wafting through the air. A waiter shows you to a table and gives you a papyrus with the menu, suggesting, 'Try our dish of the day: sea urchins with honey and a garnish of mushrooms, followed by fricassée of roses with barley beer.'

On mature reflection, and seeing there's nothing lighter on offer, such as casserole of wild boar, you say, 'Right, I'll take the dish of the day!'

You made a wise decision: the meal is delicious. You pay 50 sestertii for bed and board. It's quite expensive, but there's no such thing as a free dinner; *deduct the money from your Adventure Slab.* After a good night's

sleep you are as fit as ever, or even fitter. *Add 1 point to your Fighting Fitness score.* You do the rest of the journey at a good speed. At last Rome comes into view . . .

● Go to **70**.

54

'Oh, that's easy!'

Can your number be divided by 9, and do the digits add up to 18?

● Yes. Go to **101**.
● No. Go to **71**.

55

The dog flinches in terror. He has never smelt anything of the kind before. He goes to cower in a corner. That's all to the good; you can easily get by.

● Go to **74**.

56

Which amphora will you choose?
● The one on the left. Go to **65**.
● The one on the right. Go to **116**.
● Neither. Go to **84**.

57

One of the Romans turns and asks you point-blank, 'Heard the latest story?'

● Go to **102**.

58

Oh dear . . . there's a whole crowd behind that gladiator. No doubt about it, this has to be an ambush. *Your opponent has a Fighting Fitness score of 8.*

● If you win, go to **137**.
● If you lose, go to **79**.

59

'Caius Fatuous? I've just seen him pass by . . . but I think he was leaving.'
- Go and brood on your disappointment at **78**.

60

The servant who opened the door has gone out through a room which is full of all kinds of clothes: togas, tunics, sandals. If you like you can put on a toga and a pair of sandals, unless you have already done so. *These clothes do not count as an object, and they put your Charm score up by 2 points.*
- Go on to **89**, or go and join the party at **82**.

61

Amazing! A Herculean meal! It's a long time since you had such a feast. What's more, the innkeeper has given you one of his best rooms. After an excellent and well-deserved night's rest, it's time for you to set off again and settle the bill. *Deduct 30 sestertii from the contents of your purse (and it was a bargain!).*
- Go to **70**.

62

So here you are in a corner, or rather at the door.
- *If your Secondary Aptitude is for poetry, you can read the Roman poets.* Go to **120**.
- A metal chain with a handle is fixed to the wall. If you pull it, go to **112**.
- Maybe it would be better not to let anyone know you're here. Go to **72**.

63

'This is the problem:
  "Lucius, Octavius and Julius are playing slablets (the forerunner of cards). At the end of the game Lucius has twice as many slablets as Octavius and three times more than Julius. As you may know, games are played with 55 slablets. How many slablets does Octavius have?"'
- If you can give an answer, go to **86**.
- If not, go to **71**.

64

You can now make out a few words: 'dolmen', 'menhir', and 'Gaulish'. Then, all of a sudden, the group bursts out laughing.
- You must get closer. Go to **57**.
- Otherwise, go to **48**, or go back to **82**.

65

The Roman opens the amphora and tastes the contents. Then he turns to you and says, 'Well done! This is exactly what we needed.'
- As his companions hold out their cups, you carry on with your investigation, asking a number of questions at **118**.

66

This is easy! The faithful potion works as well as ever. But have you forgotten what your mission was? You were supposed to enquire DISCREETLY into the case of the counterfeit menhirs. What induced you to act so stupidly? It's your bad luck, because you've failed, and YOUR ADVENTURE IS OVER.

67

Take to your heels, and run the other way. But unfortunately for you, Bulimix (his name) is a very fit dog. He chases you so far that you have no chance of going to the aid of Doublehelix. YOUR ADVENTURE IS OVER.

68

'It's the story of a Gaulish tourist who goes to Gerg – I mean Alesia! – and hears a papyrus boy shouting, "Incredible! Read all about it! Sensational swindle, two hundred Gaulish tourists duped!" The Gaul buys a papyrus and unrolls it. He can't believe his eyes! It's completely blank. The papyrus boy starts shouting louder than ever. "Incredible! Read all about it! Sensational swindle, two hundred and one Gaulish tourists duped!"'

Did your story make the Romans laugh? *Take a test of Charm (difficulty 2).*
● If you succeed and the Romans roar with laughter, go to **130**.
● If the Romans don't so much as smile, go to **95**.

69

Seeing you approach, the old man holds out a curious object to you. It is a crystal ball, the sort used for auguries. Then he asks:

'Would you like your future told?'
● Why not? Sounds interesting. Go to **133**.
● You have enough problems already: no point cherishing illusions. You leave the old man and go back to **78**.

70

Thanks to the directions Getafix gave you, you easily find a villa with a brass plate on one of the walls saying SPURIUS VIRUS MEDICUS. You see two doors.
● Choose one and go to the number of the paragraph on the door.

71

'I can see you're one of those Gauls who think brute force is everything. See where that gets you! There's more to life than biceps-building and wild boar. I'll tell you something – at the siege of Alesia, Centurion Indecorus said to me one morning, he said . . .'
● If this Roman is as long-winded as Geriatrix when he gets going on Gergovia, the story will take all day. Scuttle off to **78**.

72

The door opens easily, and now your troubles begin. A fierce dog, probably a Gothic Shepherd, rushes at you, foaming at the mouth. You're in trouble, particularly as he looks like putting the bite on you. He obviously hates people to come in without knocking first.
● You try to placate him with food. Go to **80**.
● You have no food on you. Go to **67**.

73

You are close to the reclining room, where conviviality reigns, as witness the many empty amphoras lying about.

'I hope the gods will look favourably upon my entrance into this rather grand room.'

The old man covers the crystal ball with his hands, saying, 'By Jupiter and Pluto. By Mercury and Juno. May the gods be with you.'

The gods will now speak. *Throw the dice.*
● *If you throw 1 or 2*, you are under the protection of both Jupiter and Toutatis. Go to **121**.
● *If you throw 3 or 4*, you are under the protection of both Mercury and Belenos. Go to **92**.
● *If you throw 5 or 6*, where can the gods have gone? Alone and abandoned, go to **108**.

74

Here is a plan of Spurius Virus's house. All sorts of people may be met here, as in every self-respecting Roman house. *To visit it and make some interesting new acquaintances, go to the paragraphs numbered on the plan opposite.*
● You can move freely around the villa, using the clues you will unearth in the course of your visit. Go to **90** to enter.

ROMAN VILLA

You have to pay in advance here. The innkeeper gives you a suspicious glance as he holds out an imperious hand. *Quick, deduct 10 sestertii from your personal fortune before he turns nasty.* Whether it was the toad soup, the rat terrine, the bed of pebbles with a mattress of damp straw or what, you didn't sleep a wink all night. You are very weary, and you set off for Rome feeling distinctly under the weather. *Deduct 1 point from your Fighting Fitness score.*
- Go to **70**.

76

'Ah, there you are at last!' says the servant. 'And none too soon! To think that since Alesia it takes six months to find a Gaulish slave! You might have let us know you were coming!'
- Go to **122**.

77

'Welcome to Wheelerdealus, a real Good Samaritan, where you can find anything. I'm delighted to see you. Gaulish tourists are thin on the ground. The last to come to Rome was called Vercingetorix, and he didn't have much time to go shopping. I sell all sorts of things, specialising in food. Anything here interest you? I buy anything edible too. You've come a long way . . . no doubt you have some Gaulish speciality or other with you?'
- To buy whatever you want, go to **50**.
- To sell something, go to **85**.
- To leave the shop, go to **70**.

Make up your mind, because it's draughty in this peristyle, and you don't want to catch cold.
- If you think you have enough information to leave Spurius Virus's house, leave at **145**.
- The man seated at **69** may be able to help you.

- Sniff, sniff! It smells good over there. Go to **98**.
- The sound of the party you heard is coming from **123**.

The gladiator didn't look like the genuine article. He was wearing tin armour and carrying a papyrus-mâché sword. All the same, you didn't manage to beat him. What's become of the gilded youth of Gaul, once Vercingetorix's pride and joy? So far as you're concerned, YOUR ADVENTURE IS OVER.

80

What do you offer him? Take a good look at your Adventure Slab.
- The fish from the village? Go to **55**.
- Dried meat? Go to **49**.

You look rather shifty, spoon in hand; that doesn't keep you from going over to three very tasty-looking dishes.
- Will you have some soup? Go to **110**.
- A piece of cake? Go to **134**.
- Or if you sold any food to Wheelerdealus, you have a third choice: pork pie. Go to **52**.

82

Here's the atrium, a large room open to the sky, with the impluvium in the middle of it. On the right, beside this square basin, three Romans are talking and gesticulating, but from where you are you can't hear a thing.
- Go nearer to them at **64**.
- You have no time to waste. Things sound lively at **48**.
- A little fresh air would do you good. Go to **87**.
- Well, if you've found what you were after, you can go out at **145** and embark on further adventures.

83

HAHAHA!

Phew! After a few moments' hesitation, the Romans relax. They realise you were giving up the fight. One of them even smiles and asks, 'Why did you knock our friend Lapidus about?'

'He attacked me,' you stammer.

'You don't understand, Gaul!'

● Don't you think you've made enough of a mess of things already? Go back to **78**.

● No, but you'd like to understand. Go to **115**.

84

It would be better not to meet the Romans who sent you down to the cellar just now. Skirting the walls is all very well, but it's a tricky business. *Making your way through the dark unnoticed is a test of Skill (difficulty 2).*

● If you succeed, flee to **78**, and don't enter that room again.

● If not, pluck up your courage and go to **144**.

85

Wheelerdealus says he's very interested in anything from distant Armorica. He offers you:

● 20 sestertii for a Gaulish anvil. (Need we hammer it home? These Romans are crazy!)

● 40 sestertii for a musical instrument.

● 500 sestertii for a tonic (e.g. a dose of magic potion). Take the sestertii for anything you sell Wheelerdealus.

Enter the deal on your Adventure Slab.

● You've sold what you wanted to, and the conversation carries on where you left off at **77**.

● You still have something edible to sell. Go to **51**.

86

Can your answer be divided by five, and do the digits add up to 6?

● Yes. Go to **113**.

● No. Go to **71**.

87

Careful now, Justforkix! There, you've walked straight into the pool of water in the atrium. The Romans surrounding it, startled, stop talking. A hefty Nubian slave comes over and asks, 'What are you doing in there? Where do you think you are?'

● If you try to reply, go to **96**.

● Stunned by your own stupidity, you prefer to keep humbly silent. Go to **129**.

88

Listening carefully to your story, Spurius Virus has nodded his head several times. At last he murmurs, 'Yes, I know all that. The names of Bogus Litmus and Caius Fatuous are often heard here. Bogus Litmus is a rich merchant with great influence in the Senate. He's demanding stiff penalties for anyone caught trafficking in counterfeit menhirs. You probably know more about Caius Fatuous. He once met Asterix and Obelix when they visited Rome. I've an idea he's been invited today. Anyway, take this.'

Spurius Virus offers you a scroll, continuing, 'It's a false identity papyrus which will help you if you run into any patrols.' *Enter it on your Adventure Slab. It counts as an object.*

As you listen to Spurius Virus, you notice a Roman lying on a couch at the back of the reclining room, and looking intently at you.

● He may have some information, who knows? Go to **99**.

● You must find Caius Fatuous quickly. There's no time to lose. Go to **78**.

89

You have just entered the servants' dormitory. The oldest of them comes towards you, looking surprised.

'What can we do for you?'

● This is a tricky situation. You enlighten him. 'I'm Gaulish. I'm not used to Roman villas. I was looking for the vestibulum, and I must have gone the wrong way.' Go to **82**.

● At the sight of the servant you realise this would be an ideal way of seeing round the villa without arousing any suspicion. Taking your chance, you say airily, 'My name's Justforkix, and I've come from Gaul to be a servant here.' Go to **76**.

 90

The party is in full swing. What a racket! You see groups of Romans here and there talking animatedly. It's not going to be easy to find Spurius Virus without attracting attention.

● Go to **82**.

● Go into **60**.

91

A Roman comes over, red in the face with anger.

'I recognise that toga! It's my summer toga. I left it in the vestibulum!'

Roman laws come down hard on people caught with their hands in . . . the toga. YOUR ADVENTURE IS OVER.

92

The reclining room is full of Romans talking in small groups. It's hard to find an individual in this crowd. You might as well look for a pilum in a haystack. It's time to take a decision:

● You question people at random. Go to **118**.

● Why not try talking to that Roman stuffing jam down his throat on the couch at the back? Go to **99**.

● Without any further clues, it might be better to give up – for now. Go to **78**.

 93

The Roman who told you the story taps your shoulder.

'Well, my cheerful friend, know any good stories?'

Of course you've heard any amount of stories in Lutetia, good and bad.

● If you decide to tell the story of the legionary and the two lions, go to **107**.

● If you'd rather tell the story of the Gaulish papyrus, go to **68**.

● If you discreetly tell no story at all, go to **111**.

94

The conversation continues. This is a chance not to be missed. In your most genial tones you ask, 'Between friends, surely you're not really too bothered about these counterfeit menhirs?'

This question has the Roman in a quandary. He does not reply. You insist. You'd better turn on your legendary charm. *Take a test of Charm (difficulty 3).*

● If you succeed, go to **141**.

● If you fail, go to **126**.

 95

Hm! Not exactly a warm reception. Either you don't tell stories very well, or it wasn't a very good story. In any case, the Romans look disappointed, and don't seem inclined to listen to you any longer.

● Go to **48**.

96

In this tricky situation, it is important that you hit the right note.

● If you decide on an answer which at least sounds logical, go to **114**.

● If you decide deep thought is better, go to **109**.

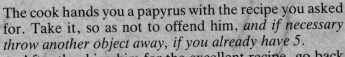

97

The cook hands you a papyrus with the recipe you asked for. Take it, so as not to offend him, *and if necessary throw another object away, if you already have 5*.
● After thanking him for the excellent recipe, go back to **78**.

98

Mmm, something smells good! But who knows what's cooking in these kitchens? Though it all seems very appetising, you decide to take a closer look.
● There's food for thought here. Go to **81**.
● You won't find the answer to your problems here. Go back to **78**.

99

'Come here, Gaul! You look as if you've lost something.'
This Roman seems trustworthy, but you must be on your guard.
● You reply, 'I'm looking for a man called Caius Fatuous.' Go to **59**.
● You try, 'I want to buy a menhir as a souvenir, but I can't find one anywhere.' The Roman replies at **138**.

COME HERE, GAUL!

100

Phew! Your heart and your purse are both lighter.
● Try to be a little more economical at **92**.

101

The correct answer is three hundred and seventy-eight.
● If you didn't get it right, hurry to **71**.
● If you got it right, go to **124**.

102

'What latest story?'
'Why, the latest Gaulish story! It's a really good one! There's this Gaul repainting his dolmen, and his friend says to him, "You hold the brush and I'll move the menhir."'
Ho, ho! The storyteller's friends fall about laughing.
● These Romans are idiots! It doesn't make you laugh at all. Go to **48**.
● You join in the general amusement. Go to **93**.

103

Over the Roman's shoulder, you read: 'Three Gauls, a fat one, a small one and a bard, all stuffed with magic potion except for the fat one, who fell into it when he was a baby, attacked a Roman camp. In the time it took the fat one to thump two Romans, the small Gaul thumped one Roman. The bard had his lyre in one hand, so he thumped only one legionary in the time it took the small Gaul to finish off two. At the end of this memorable fight, the small Gaul had knocked out a hundred and eight legionaries. How many legionaries were there in the camp?' (Obviously not a single legionary had escaped the brave Gaulish warriors!)
● This story revives certain memories, but it would be better to ask for an explanation. Go to **117**.
● These Romans are crazy! Better not get across them. Go to **78**.
● Can you work out the answer? Try it at **54**.

104

The first thing you see is a gladiator advancing on you. What on earth is going on? By Belisama, that gladiator looks a tough customer. Quick, you must do something!
- Hold out your hand as a sign of friendship, and go to meet him at **127**.
- Prepare to fight at **58**.
- Withdraw at **142**.

105

Is it sensible to have a fourth helping? No, particularly not when you have such an important mission to carry out. Haven't you a thought to spare for your poor father, condemned to Roman prison rations? You are a heartless son, and YOUR ADVENTURE IS OVER.

106

The man turns round, asking, 'What do you want?'
'I'm looking for a friend, Spurius Virus, and I wondered if he was here.'
'No. As you can see, I'm alone with my books and my problems.'
'Your problems?'
- Why not find out about his problems? Go to **63**.
- You've got enough problems of your own. Go to **78**.

107

'Two hungry lions are chatting in the middle of the desert. One of the lions suddenly sees a legionary in full armour coming their way. "Good," says the lion, "this looks like dinner!" "Bother!" says the other lion. "Tinned food again!"'
Do the Romans have a sense of humour? To find out, *take a test of Charm (difficulty 4)*.
- If they roar with laughter, go to **130**.
- If you don't even raise a smile, go to **95**.

108

A group of party-goers is barring the way, but you might gather some information from them.
'Could you tell me where to find Spurius Virus?'
'Looking for good old Spurius?' says one of the Romans. 'I'll tell you if you'll do me a small service. Our friend Virus has some amphoras of Burdigala wine of the year 162 in his cellar. An excellent year. Go and fetch us one, and I'll tell you what you want to know.'
- Not only does this sound dangerous, but who knows if he will keep his word? You'd do better to refuse. Go to **78**.
- When you've started you might as well finish. You go off to the cellar at **139**.

109

'A metre deep! I was right! I bet my girl-friend Hydrophobia that the pool wasn't as deep as all that – although on the other hand, the pen of my aunt . . . ' Your explanation is a bit complicated, but you might take them in. *This test of Charm (difficulty 4) is not an easy one; luckily you've faced such problems before.*
- If you succeed, go to **48**, wet but convincing.
- If not, silence greets your explanation. Go to **131**.

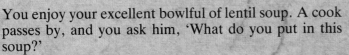

110

You enjoy your excellent bowlful of lentil soup. A cook passes by, and you ask him, 'What do you put in this soup?'

'Vegetables, noodles and water.'
'Where does the water come from?'
'The sacred river Tiber. It has a Roman aroma, get it?'
- Armed with this information, go to **132**.
- 'I'll have another helping.' Go to **105**.

111

The Romans look glum. One of them says, 'Gauls used to be better company in the old days. Soon they'll have forgotten how to tell a funny story at all.'
- Taking no more notice of you, they go back to their conversation. Go to **48**.

112

You have hardly touched the handle when you hear a bell ring. The door opens and a servant appears in the doorway.

'What do you want?' he asks.
'I'm looking for Spurius Virus. Tell him I've come from the druid Getafix.'
'Just a moment, please.'
Several minutes later, the servant comes back and invites you in. 'My master's giving a reception. You're welcome to join the party, and you're sure to come across him somewhere.'
- The servant withdraws. Go to **74**.

113

The right answer is fifteen.
- If you didn't get it right, go to **71**, quick.
- Hooray! You got it right! Go to **124**.

114

You stammer, 'Please forgive my boldness. I only wanted to take a bath, just to freshen up. No harm in that, I hope.'
You look anxiously at the Romans facing you. Will they believe you?
- If you have a toga, go to **91**.
- If not, go to **125**.

115

'We Romans enjoy a good gladiatorial combat. However, gladiators' costumes have hardly changed at all in two hundred years. One of my friends, Lapidus, has designed new outfits, and he's showing them today.'

Taking you by the shoulder, the man continues, in very friendly tones, 'Somehow you remind me of two Gauls I knew. Their names were Asterix and Obelix. Have you ever met them? Real warriors, they were!'
● 'Yes, of course. They're my best friends at home in the village.' Go to **94**.
● You can never be too careful. 'No, those names mean nothing to me. Thanks for the delightful fashion parade.' And you parade off to **78**.

116

'Here, there's your amphora.'
'Let's have a taste and see if it's the right wine . . . Burdigala 112! YUK! That year was sheer vinegar! If you're being funny, Gaul, I'll . . .'
● Get out, fast, to **78** (and you'd better not come back this way).

117

Take a dose of magic potion if you like. You can never be too careful. Tap the Roman on his left shoulder to attract his attention.
● If you've drunk some potion, go to **119**.
● If not, go to **106**.

118

To question those present at random, throw the dice twice and add your number of Charm points. If your score comes to over 20, you succeed in finding Spurius Virus. You can have up to three tries, but you can give up before the third.
● If you have found Spurius Virus, go to **88**.
● If you haven't found him after three tries, go to **136**.
● If you have given up, sit down for a moment and think. Then go back to **92** and try a different choice.

119

Your friendly tap has rammed the Roman ten centimetres or more into the ground. What a social gaffe! The master of the house comes along, and is horrified to see the extent of the damage.
'Arrest him!' he shouts to his servants.
They try to catch you, but without success. Thanks to the magic potion, you're brimming with vitality. However, you realise Spurius Virus will be paying for the damage, and he won't want to see your face here any more. YOUR ADVENTURE IS OVER.

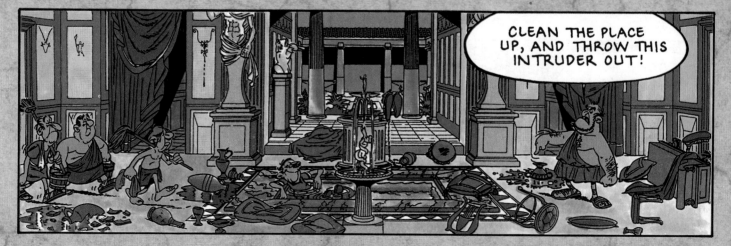

120

No doubt about it, you're looking at an inscription saying CAVE CANEM, partly worn away by the weather.
● Go to **62** – and beware of the dog!

121

CRAASH! Look where you're going – you've just bumped into a Roman. He is not pleased.

'Where are you going so fast, young Gaul? When you cast auguries without looking far enough ahead you're bound to end up with a bruise or so. It's not the gods' fault! My name's Spurius Virus. I don't think I've had the pleasure of meeting you.'

'My name's Justforkix, and I have a message from Getafix.'
● Your conversation continues at **88**.

122

Did you catch what he said to you? He said SLAVE, not SERVANT. On hearing that, you ask him, 'What am I to do?'

It is the captain of one of Spurius Virus's three galleys who replies, briefly, 'Row.'

Poor Justforkix. YOUR ADVENTURE IS OVER. However, a new, naval career lies ahead.

123

Approaching the triclinium, you hear shouts and applause, followed by sounds you can't identify. There seems to be great merriment behind that curtain.
● Take a deep breath and step forward to push it aside at **104**.

124

The old man's face lights up.

'Well done, Gaul! Welcome to this library.'

He takes you over to the shelves and tells you all about their contents. He speaks volumes, but you have to be patient if you want to stay in his good books.

'You're the sort of lively, enterprising young fellow I like. Choose one of these books. I'll make you a present of it.'

The pile of books he points to contains:

– *Ancient Egyptian*, by Bogus Litmus.
– *Novella Culina*, by Bocus.
– *The Circus and the Games*, by Barnum and Bailus.
– *The Laws of Rome*, by Publicus Prosecutus.
● *Choose one of these books if you like. Enter it on your list of objects.*
● But you still have a lot to learn. Go to **78**.

125

The Romans look totally surprised, and your appearance really puts the lid on it. You clamber out, feeling as wet as you look. Well, you wanted to be soaked in Roman culture, didn't you? *Deduct 2 points from your Charm score*.
● Go to **48**.

126

Caius Fatuous, for it is he, hands you a cup full of a delicious-looking liquid.

'Here, Gaul, have a drop of goat's milk while I give you my opinion.'

Yum, yum! It tastes as good as it looks!

'If you ask me, it's certain that . . .'

The rest of Caius Fatuous's opinion is lost in the mists of slumber.
● The sleeping draught wears off at **151**.

127

Things are not always what they seem! The gladiator withdraws several steps, and you see a dozen or so Romans . . . who start applauding loudly.

'Good show, Lapidus!'

'Splendid idea, really original!'

'Positively Gaulish, that outfit!'

'Let's see the next model!' chant the Romans.

● You stick around to find out what it's all about at **115**.

● Bad luck! And you thought you'd slip in discreetly . . . Go back to **78**.

128

The walls are covered with shelves, the shelves are covered with papyri, and the papyri are covered with dust. This must be Spurius Virus's library. An old man, bent over his desk, is sitting with his back to you.

● You are discreet and don't disturb him. Go to **78**.

● Curiosity gets the better of you. You try to read over his shoulder. Go to **103**.

● Ahem! Your little cough will attract his attention. Go to **106**.

129

You are soaked from head to foot. Cold water has been poured on your plans, but you wave aside a torrent of Roman insults. Seething with rage, Spurius Virus has you thrown out. YOUR ADVENTURE IS OVER.

130

'Well, young fellow, you're a cheerful sort. Where are you from?'

'Lutetia.'

'Lutetia! You're lucky, living in such a go-ahead city! What are they talking about in Lutetia these days?'

A chance not to be missed! 'There's a lot of talk about trafficking in counterfeit menhirs. Have you heard of that here?'

'Yes, of course.' And the Roman starts talking. But he knows no more than you do. However, your keen ear happens to pick up a whispered comment by one of the other two Romans.

'One man who won't have anything to complain of is Bogus Litmus.'

The Romans prepare to leave the atrium. Curiosity leads you to ask one last question.

● 'Who's Bogus Litmus?' Go to 135.

● No point in wasting any more time. You leave them. Go to 48.

131

A centurion on duty, attracted by the noise, comes over.

'Just what I wanted. I was wondering about the depth of a galley's hold. You come with me, and we'll measure it together.'

Swiftly, you seize your gourd of magic potion and attack. 'Come on, then, Roman!' Then, too late, you remember the words of Getafix. 'Take care not to get the gourd wet, because if the potion is at all diluted it loses all its power.' YOUR ADVENTURE IS OVER.

- It would be a shame to waste any of such a good cake. Go to **105**.
- You ask for the recipe for Impedimenta. Go to **97**.
- You try something else to eat, at **81**.

No doubt about it, a little snack does you good. *Add 1 point to your Fighting Fitness score while you are in this house.*
- Go back to **78**, and don't come into the kitchen again.

The old man stares at the crystal ball and says, 'I see an eventful future ahead of you. There is someone dear to you who is now a prisoner and whom you wish to rescue.'

This is the moment to try and take advantage of the situation. 'Would you ask the gods to help me in my quest?'

'You are noble and brave. I will!'
- He asks the gods their advice at **73**.

135

'Bogus Litmus is a rich merchant dealing in stones and houses. He's very well known around here.'

'Never heard of him myself.'

'Haven't you?' says the Roman. 'He built the docklands villas and the Pompey II Centre. And he sold decorative stones and souvenirs before the menhir fashion hit Rome. He's very influential in the Senate.'

The Roman's voice is dropping to a whisper, as if he feared being overheard. Anyone would think the walls had ears!
- Glad to have this information, you say goodbye. Go to **48**.

134

This is a very good cake, although rather rich. An almond cake.
- One more slice, that's all. Go to **132**.

The first group showed you the door. A Roman in the second group asked you to go to the atrium and see if he was there. The third group were so busy discussing the games in the circus next day, they hardly noticed you.
- Go back to **78**, and don't return to this inhospitable place.

137

As soon as you have finished with the gladiator, and before you even have time to get your breath back, all the other Romans present fall on you, looking ferocious.
- 'They'll see what you're made of.' Face them at **140**.
- 'They'll find out what this drink's made of.' *Deduct 1 dose of magic potion.* Fight them at **66**.
- You prefer to throw down your arms and appease them. Talk to them at **83**. (They'll take some persuading.)

138

'I can give you some interesting information for 50 sestertii – the cost of living's terrible these days.'
- No one fools you that way. Go to **78**.
- O.K. *Deduct 50 sestertii from your fortune.* Go to **143**.

139

This could be dangerous . . . suppose you fall down the steps. Suppose a servant finds you . . . suppose you pick the wrong amphora . . . oh, buck up! You've gotta lotta amphora, right?
- Pluck up your courage and go down to **56**.
- Give up and go back to **84**.

140

Where are you? In a spot, obviously. What was the point of Getafix working his fingers to the bone to make you some potion? Now you're flattened under a heap of Romans, and you'll have heaps of trouble coming. YOUR ADVENTURE IS OVER.

141

'I like you. Come and see me tomorrow at the games, and then I'll tell you more. Here, take this.' *Enter an invitation slablet on your Adventure Slab. It doesn't count as an object.*
- Go back to **78**.

142

You just have time to see Romans on both sides of the curtain. This must be a trap. Quick, you'd better escape while you can.
- Flee to **78**.

143

The Roman comes over and whispers in your ear. 'I know someone who can tell you more. He's called Grampus, and he works in the arena. Go and see him and tell him I sent you. My name's Minus Sinus.'
'How will I get in? I don't know anyone.'
'Here, take this invitation slablet. It's valid for tomorrow, and it will get you in.' *Enter the slablet on your Adventure Slab if you keep it (it doesn't count as an object).*
- Thank him and go to **78**.

144

You go over to the Romans, not feeling too happy. They look at you with a smile at first, but on seeing that you are empty-handed they frown.
'Hey, haven't you forgotten something, Gaul?'
This is getting serious.
- You say apologetically, 'Oh, was it Burdigala 162 you wanted? I'll go back for it.' The way down to the cellar is at **139**.
- You look knowing and say, 'Personally, I think the Burdigala 163 is better. Here are 100 sestertii – buy yourselves an amphora and try it.' *Deduct that amount* and leave the Romans at **100**.

CHAPTER III

BREAD AND CIRCUSES

145

All Rome is talking of today's Games. Yes, the Games begin this afternoon. In the streets, small groups are converging on the arena.
● Follow the crowd towards the entry to the arena at **160**.
● The atmosphere is festive, the crowd a motley one. Why not stroll about a bit, to **154**?
● You can buy a programme for 5 sestertii at **156**.

146

Remove 2 sestertii from your purse.
   The question is, do you eat that sausage at once or do you keep it for later?
● At once. Go to **155**.
● Later. Go to **150**.

147

There is already a long queue, and a lot of Romans are waiting in barbarian file*. You must be patient. At last there are only two Romans left in front of you. But at this very moment they hang out a notice saying HOUSE FULL. The first shouts are rising to the skies. The show is beginning, but sad to say, you won't see it, even though the key to your mission is inside. YOUR ADVENTURE IS OVER.

* The barbarians went in Hun by Hun

148

All you need to know is on the slablet: you must go to the gate marked EG (no doubt for Envoys of Gaul).
● Go to **152**.

38

149

'But you'll be sure to lose your sestertii! I consider myself a good driver, but only on the roads. I can't drive a racing chariot.'

You have put all your powers of persuasion into your voice. *Take a test of Charm (difficulty 3)*.
- If you succeed in convincing Caius Fatuous, go to **153**.
- If not, he shakes his head doubtfully. Go to **157**.

150

Pocketing your sausage (*which counts as an object*), you:
- Go to the turnstiles at **160**.
- Buy a programme at **156**.

151

You come round behind bars!
- Better wait and see what happens next. Go to **159**.
- This is no time for subtlety. Better take a swig of potion and go to **169**!

152

The small door opens and a head looks in.
'Who are you?'
'My name's Justforkix, and I'm expected.'
'Who sent you?'
'I have a complimentary slablet.'
'Let's see it.'

A hand takes your slablet and immediately invites you in. You are inside the circus.
- As you follow the man to **158**, you just have time to see a carved inscription saying EG: ENTRY OF THE GLADIATORS.

153

'Justforkix, I'm convinced, I'm glad to say, seeing I've put all my money on your opponent! Right, off we go!'
- You have no choice. Go to **170**.

154

A compatriot of yours is offering Arvernian sausages for sale, 2 sestertii each.
- You ought to do your bit for Gaulish trade, and besides, you're feeling a little peckish, as Obelix might say. You buy a sausage at **146**.
- This is no time for idling about. Go back to **145**.

155

That was a mistake – the sausage is very salty, and it means that you'll be thirsty for several hours. Your mouth feels dry *and you lose 3 points of Fighting Fitness while you are in the arena. Enter it on your Adventure Slab*.
- You decide to go to the box office. There's a queue waiting at **160**.
- Ask for a programme at **156**.

156

What a great programme!
- This you really must see! Go to **160**.
- There's no hurry. Take a little stroll to **154**.

157

'Are you telling me you can only drive a one horse-power chariot?'
'That's right.' (Phew!)
- Go and see if you've fooled Caius Fatuous at **153**.

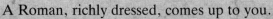

158

A Roman, richly dressed, comes up to you.

'My name is Caius Fatuous. I hear you're looking for me. Well, here I am, and you're my guest. I've reserved you a splendid place for the games which are about to begin: you're going to drive in the chariot race. If you win, you'll be famous; if you lose, well, that's just too bad. It's up to you, and the best of luck! I've staked my whole fortune on the result of this race.'

Two hefty Romans you didn't notice before make you put on a charioteer's outfit, removing all your own clothes.

- You've always been a bit of a fatalist. Go to **170**.
- It's worth trying one last (rather risky) appeal. Go to **149**.

159

You don't have to wait long.

- A key turns in the lock at **158**.

160

The crowd is already gathering at the gates.

- If you have an invitation slablet, go to **148**.
- If not, you'll have to queue up at **147**.

161

You reach the Roman terraces. Spectators are waving large banners saying 'Come on Grampus' and 'Just-forkix is for the Styx.'

- Better not hang about here. Hurry to **171**.

162

A placard saying 'Arvernians for Justforkix' gives you a bit of courage. You may well need it.

- Move one space forward. Go to **171**.

163

Help! You missed, and now you have lost your pilum. The die, or rather the pilum, is cast. Only victory can save you now.

- *Cross the pilum off the drawing of the chariot.* Gallop to **171**.

164

'Come on, Grampus!'

Your chariots have reached the turn where the supporters of Grampus are standing. They start throwing their programmes on the track to encourage him. *Throw the dice to try to avoid them. If your result is less than the number of spaces you have driven you can't avoid one of the programmes. It hits you in the face.*

- All right? Go to **171**.
- Hit by a programme? Go to **188**.

165

The delirious crowd wildly applauds the winner.

- If you have won, go to **211**.
- If Grampus has won, go to **173**.

40

166

Grampus's pilum has passed between your chariot wheels . . . CRAAASH! . . . breaking the axle. Just look at the state the chariot is in. You'll be more careful another time.

● Go to **199**.

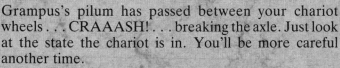

167

However, it's a fact: you've just lost one of your reins. *Cross it off the drawing.*

● That's not a disaster – yet; it's only the first rein. Go on to **191**.

● That's the second rein gone. Remember that things usually go in threes. Drive to **185**.

● That was your last rein. Curse the gods for playing such a cruel trick on you! You reflect on your bad luck at **197**.

168

Help! Those senators are rich! They've bought de luxe programmes made of solid marble. You must summon up all your skill to deal with the situation. *Take a test of Skill (difficulty 3).*

● If you succeed, go to **190**.

● If you fail, go to **198**.

169

What's happened to Getafix's gourd? Thinking it contained wine, your jailers have confiscated it.

● You resign yourself to waiting at **159**.

170

Here's the arena . . . and your opponent; Grampus, the best charioteer west of Alexandria. *First take a look at your chariot. You have a brand-new chariot, three horses and a fine spear. Then look at the track: the luck of the draw has given you the outside lane.* The referee is going over the rules again:

'As soon as the signal is given, start off, keeping to your own lane, and the first past the finishing line is the winner. You have a spear which you can throw at your opponent at any time.'

Are you ready? Each charioteer plays in turn. Your opponent begins, moving one space each turn. Then you play, throwing the dice, which tells you the maximum number of spaces you can move (for instance, if you throw 4, you can move 1, 2, 3 or 4 spaces). Unfortunately it's obvious that you aren't really used to chariot racing, and you risk danger if you drive too fast. So when you decide to move more than 3 spaces (if the throw of the dice allows it) you must consult the **Danger Slab**. This slab shows the number of the paragraph where you must go to find out what has happened to you. To do this, use the number of spaces you have moved this turn, and the letter on the space where you have landed (for instance, if you move four spaces at the start and find yourself on a space marked B, consult paragraph 178, as indicated, where 4 and B intersect). If you break anything, mark it with a cross on the plan of the chariot at the side of the track. If your Secondary Aptitude is chariot-running-in, move your chariot two spaces at once. If the book THE GAMES AND THE CIRCUS is on your Adventure Slab, you will have read it with interest, and it comes in useful; move your chariot two spaces. This advantage may be added to the previous one. If so, take no notice of the paragraph numbers. As soon as one of the rival charioteers passes the finishing line, go to **165**.

• The signal to start is given. You're off, at **171**.

SPACE \ DICE	IV	V	VI
	180	180	180
	178	180	180
	178	182	180
	210	206	176
	202	202	195
	183	179	207
	161	164	179
	210	175	195
	164	189	175
	162	174	207
	174	207	184

DANGER SLAB

GRAMPUS

JUSTFORKIX

171

Move Grampus's chariot 1 space.
● Unless Grampus has reached the finishing line, the race goes on. Your turn.

172

The handful of sand that cheat Grampus has thrown in your face momentarily blinds you. *Move only 1 space next turn*, to give yourself time to wipe your eyes and see clearly again.
● Go to **171**.

173

The referee proclaims:
'Grampus is the winner and takes first prize: a laurel wreath donated by Julius Caesar himself. Justforkix is the loser, and wins second prize, also donated by Caesar: a sea voyage on board a Roman galley.'
A generous fellow, Caesar. YOUR ADVENTURE IS OVER. Have a good trip.

174

Quick, this is your big chance! Grampus is within reach. Holding the reins in one hand, you have an opportunity of snatching up your pilum (if you still have it) and throwing it. It won't be easy, but you may succeed.
● If you'd rather not try for the moment, or if you have lost your pilum, go to **171**.
● Pick up your pilum and throw it. *This is a test of Skill, difficulty 5; don't forget to cross it off your chariot.* If you succeed, go to **187**. If not, go to **193**.

175

At the bend your troubles start. One rein slips out of your hands.
● You try to recover it. *Take a test of Skill, difficulty 4.* If

you fail, recover your balance at **209**. If you succeed, get your breath back at **171**.
● It never reins but it pours. You don't try anything. Go to **167**.

176

Look at your left wheel! The left, idiot, not the right! This is terrible . . . IT'S COMING OFF! *Don't forget to mark it on your chariot.*
● Go to **186** to inspect the damage.

177

Yes, you've skidded . . . the night life of Lutetia wasn't especially good training for acrobatics of this kind. Games in the circus are not your strong point. You need to get fit.
● Go to **173** and see what's in store for you.

178

No need to take off as if your other name was Supersonix. Show a bit of horse sense in future!
● Slow down at **171**.

179

Has Grampus drawn level? *Is the space occupied by his chariot next to yours*?
● If Grampus is level with you, go to **204**.
● If not, be cautious and go to **171**.

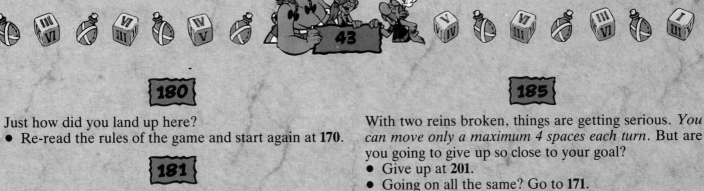

180

Just how did you land up here?
- Re-read the rules of the game and start again at **170**.

181

When the crowd realised you were going to try carrying on with only one wheel they rose to you in admiration. A tense silence falls over the arena. *You absolutely must pass this test of Skill (difficulty 4).*
- If – incredibly! – you have succeeded, continue the race at **171**, *but you cannot use 6 any more.*
- If not, the second wheel looks like coming off ... CRACK! Go to **199**.

182

Obviously Grampus is close behind you, and he has a definite plan in mind.
- If he is beside you, that is, if his chariot is on a space next to yours, he takes cowardly advantage of it to try cheating and make you swerve. You duck to avoid the blow. *Take a test of Skill, difficulty 3.* If you succeed, go to **196**. If not, go to **177**.
- If he isn't beside you, carry on the race at **171** – and watch out!

183

Holding the reins in your teeth, you have a chance of grasping your pilum and throwing it.
- If you would rather not just now, or if you have already thrown your pilum, go to **171**.
- Pick up your pilum and throw it. *This is a test of Skill, difficulty 6 (cross the pilum off the picture of your chariot).* If you succeed, go to **187**. If not, go to **163**.

184

Those must be the Gaulish seats. Shouts of 'Up with Gaul' and 'Come on, Justforkix!' ring out from them.
- Go to **171**.

185

With two reins broken, things are getting serious. *You can move only a maximum 4 spaces each turn.* But are you going to give up so close to your goal?
- Give up at **201**.
- Going on all the same? Go to **171**.

186

The other wheel looks like breaking. In fact it's bound to. It would be madness to carry on.
- Give up the race at **201**.
- You won't? Try the impossible at **181**.

187

By Belenos! You hit the bull's eye. Your pilum landed in the wheel of Grampus's chariot and broke it right off. While shouts of triumph rise from the benches of the Gaulish supporters, Grampus painfully gets to his feet. The crowd, rising, applauds you to the echo.
- Pick up the laurels of victory at **211**.

188

This really is your lucky day! You've just had a real eyeful of the programme. Are the omens good? *Throw the dice.*
- If you got a programme from one of the plebeian benches, i.e. if you threw 1, 2, or 3, go to **203**.
- If you got a senator's programme, i.e. if you threw 4, 5 or 6, go to **168**.

189

You're in a good position now. Holding the reins with one hand, you can pick up your pilum and throw it. It isn't easy, but you may succeed.
- If you would rather not just now, or if you have already thrown your pilum, go to **171**.
- Pick up your pilum and throw it. *Take a test of Skill, difficulty 4, and cross the pilum off the picture of your chariot.* If you succeed, go to **187**. If not, go to **163**.

190

This is a full programme. It was heavy reading, and you have difficulty recovering from the consequences. *Next turn you cannot move more than 3 spaces at the most.*
- Go to **171**.

191

The rein has fallen into the arena. Driving your chariot is difficult in the circumstances. *From now on you cannot move more than 5 spaces at most per turn.*
- Go to **171** (and take care).

192

Lean on the shaft and lower your head. *Throw the dice.*
- If you throw 1, 2, 3 or 4, go to **194**.
- If you throw 5 or 6, go to **171**.

193

Phew! You just missed falling, but as your chariot lurched the pilum fell from your hands. You won't be able to use it now.
- Regain control of your horses and gallop on to **171**.

194

Grampus, thinking he's well within range, has just thrown his pilum. It is flying towards you. Help! This looks serious. You must do something. *Take a test of Skill (difficulty 3).*
- If you manage to avoid the pilum, go to **205**.
- If not, go to **166**.

195

Have you seen your right wheel? You can hardly believe your eyes, but it's true . . . the wheel is rolling gently off the track, because you've just lost it. *Don't forget to cross it off your chariot.*
- Go and inspect the damage at **207**.

196

The manoeuvre surprised Grampus, *but you can't move more than 2 spaces at your next turn*.
- Go to **171**.

197

You have lost control of both your chariot and the situation. Taking risks is necessary, but you ought to think before you act . . . YOUR ADVENTURE IS OVER.

198

OUCH! That marble programme almost knocked you over. Courage! You carry on with the race as best you can. Grampus has taken advantage of it to move one space.
- Go to **171**.

199

You chariot isn't driving, it's skidding. . . how long can a chariot skid over sand? Do you really want to know?
- The reply is at **208**.

200

Poor Justforkix! Stay level with him? That's just what Grampus wants, and you will soon find out that no holds are barred in the Games at the Circus.
- Go to **172**.

201

Well, if you are going to give up at the first setback . . . as you can imagine, the Gaulish spectators are very disappointed. Two soldiers soon come to collect you. YOUR ADVENTURE IS OVER.

202

'Come on, Grampus, come on!'

Your chariots have reached that part of the track, near a bend, where Grampus's supporters are sitting. They start throwing their programmes (which you will remember are made of marble) on the track to encourage your opponent. Try to avoid them. *Throw the dice. If your result is equal to or greater than 5, you avoid an accident.*
- All right? Go to **171**.
- Hit by a programme? Go to **188**.

203

Luckily the programme was a cheap one, weighing no more than a sheet of papyrus. Imagine what it would be like if you'd got the de luxe marble programme!
- Carry on with the race at **171**.

204

That cheat Grampus has thrown sand in your face. So that's his Roman game!
- If you accelerate to avoid him, gallop to **192**.
- If you slow down, brake at **196**.
- You decide to stay level with him to defy him. Drive to **200**.

205

Grampus lets out a yell of rage . . . and disappointment. Meanwhile he has lost speed, *so move forward 1 space.*
- Go and laugh at him at **171**.

206

Grampus makes for your chariot with the clear intention of overturning it. Trusting in its manoeuvrability, you try to avoid the collision. *This is a test of Skill, difficulty 4.*
- If you swerve, take a deep breath and go to **171**.
- If you can't avoid the collision, go to **199**.

207

CRACK! A wheel has given way, with a sinister noise. *Enter the damage on your chariot.* Is it the first to go?
- Yes. Try to save the situation, still rather a serious one, at **181**.
- Yes, but things are getting hot enough already and you don't want to run risks. Better give up at **201**.
- No, it's the second wheel, and you don't have a spare. So you're really going spare at **199**.

208

Ask a silly question . . . Your race comes to a noisy end. Acclaimed by the crowd, Grampus raises his arms aloft in triumph.
- Go to **173** to see your opponent triumph.

209

Phew! A little further and you'd be biting the dust. You just have time to get back on board your chariot, and Grampus has seized his chance to accelerate. *You can't move more than 3 spaces next turn.*
- Go to **167**.

210

Careful! Speed is intoxicating but dangerous, as you ought to know. CRACK! Your toga gets caught in a wheel and tears. Luckily it wasn't top quality cloth, because you're not the stuff of which heroes are made. You have to slow down to adjust it, *so you can't move more than 5 spaces next turn.*
- Be more careful; go to **171**.

CHAPTER IV

THE CITY OF ROME

The arena echoes with applause. The crowd rises, cheering loudly and soon all that can be seen is a confused mass of people. The Roman Security Cohorts intervene to calm things down.

Now then, Justforkix, don't let this distract you – you still have a mission to carry out.
- 'And now for you, Caius Fatuous!' Go to **220**.

What a fight, by Toutatis! Your opponent is a big, hefty fellow. And the Roman with the red towel seems to have evaporated, perhaps because of the heat.
- Don't come back here. Go back, reeling, to **250**, or try to be more diplomatic next time.

Caius Fatuous found it very difficult to part with his 5000 sestertii, but, shedding tears and grinding his teeth he does so. *Enter your new fortune on your Adventure Slab*. Thanks to this money, you'll be able to help Doublehelix.
- You decide to return to Lutetia at **266**.

- You must continue your enquiries in Rome. The solution to the riddle must certainly be here. You see the entrance to an alley at **291**.

A sombre expression, a stern look, all those small details indicating that a Roman who doesn't like being disturbed for nothing (or for not much) is deep in thought. No doubt about it, you've missed a chance here. Go out again and try to be more diplomatic next time.
- If this is the second time you've had such a reaction from a Roman, go to **314**.
- You know enough. Leave the temple at **271**.
- If you've just made an offering, try a speech at **305**.
- If you've just made a speech, try making an offering at **283**.

Yes, here you are, outside the arena. *Now you must choose which way to go. You can't retreat or change direction (has anyone ever seen a Gaul lose his way or refuse to fight?).*
- Refer to the paragraphs with numbers along the route you choose.

216

Deduct a dose from your Adventure Slab.
- Immersed in your thoughts, you wonder whether to go for an early bath, and return to **250**.

217

'The cost of living here is high, and rising all the time. How much do your offer?' asks the Roman, fixing greedy eyes on you and waiting for your reply.
- 50 sestertii. Go to **228**.
- 100 sestertii. Go to **281**.
- 500 sestertii. Go to **262**.
- 1000 sestertii. Go to **237**.
- You prefer a muscular reply. Clench your fists and go to **264**.
- All things considered, you'd better get out of here.

218

Well, you're a cool customer and no mistake! You've just plunged into a pool of icy water.
- If you've already passed through the sudatorium, go to **223**.
- If not, go to **259**.

219

The potion has proved its worth once again! After a short, energetic interlude, the patrol is in bad shape and the ground is littered with slightly worn sandals. You can continue your journey, but avoid other patrols. And take care: Roman law is harsh, and you're still a long way from your journey's end.
- Continue on your way (*deducting the dose of potion*).

220

'W . . . well done, Justforkix.'
Your old friend Caius Fatuous isn't very happy.
'I think you must have lost quite a lot of sestertii,' you remark, retrieving your things (*don't forget to record the fact on your Adventure Slab*).

Suddenly Caius Fatuous's face clears, or rather it assumes a cunning expression, which is a bad sign.
'I've had a good idea, Gaul. Let's go and see the people I was betting with and admit that you're one of those indomitable Gauls stuffed with magic potion. Then I can get the bets cancelled because of doping.'
- 'Fine, but I'd like you to answer a few questions.' You ask them at **229**.
- 'Fine, but I want 5000 sestertii for my trouble.' Go to **213**.
- 'No, I won't. What do you take me for? Anyway, I think I hear someone knocking at the door already. Goodbye.' Leave Caius Fatuous and go to **227**.

221

'Ave. I'm a friend of Caius Fatuous.'
'How's old Caius, then? You've turned up at just the right time. I could do with someone to lend a hand. There's a full cargo to unload after dark, same as usual.'
'How about the patrols?'
'Don't worry, Bogus Litmus is in the know.'
'What's the name of the ship?'

HURRY UP AND GET THE STUFF UNLOADED, YOU LAZY LOT! YOU'LL MAKE ME MISS THE TIDE!

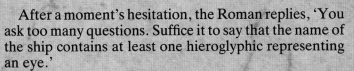
After a moment's hesitation, the Roman replies, 'You ask too many questions. Suffice it to say that the name of the ship contains at least one hieroglyphic representing an eye.'

As if aware of having said a little too much, the Roman leaves the massage room.

● You leave too.

● Why not have a spot of massage yourself? The table and the masseur are at **282**.

222

You are facing a big building. Carved over the door are the words BATHS OLIVUS.

● The entrance to the baths is at **250**.

● This takes the biscuit! You'll try the Senate instead. Take the road right to **299**.

● Or take the road left to **285**.

223

Brrr . . . after the steam bath, the ice-cold water is quite a shock. You speak to the stranger.

'Tactac . . . tactac . . . tactac . . . glagla . . . tactac . . . glaglagla . . . tac . . .' Your teeth, chattering away, are conducting this conversation by themselves.

● You can't articulate properly. Go and warm up somewhere else.

224

'Oh, go to the sudatorium* and see if I'm there. I've got other things to do!'

All you can do after such a warm welcome is clear out.

*Steam room

225

No sooner have you taken a dose of potion than the centurion cries, 'Walking while over the limit! You're for it, laddie!'

● There is a terrific punch-up at **219**!

226

'I don't know anyone of that name here. You'd better try the Senate.'

● You say goodbye and leave.

227

It was rather unkind, leaving Caius Fatuous to the mercy of his creditors like that. However, it's too late now to remember that he was your only source of information. YOUR ADVENTURE IS OVER.

228

'Is that all? Not very generous, are you?' *All the same, deduct 50 sestertii from your personal funds.* 'However, I'll show you I'm not ungrateful: the ship you want is in port. Go down to the docks, and good luck, sestertius-pincher!'

● That's something, anyway. Go and think it over outside the baths at **250**.

● You still have a few sestertii which might be useful. Go back to **217**.

229

When you question him closely, Caius Fatuous admits that he has often 'lent' gladiators out for heavy manual labour. They had to unload the cargoes (no doubt consisting of Egyptian stones) from ships anchored in the Tiber and take the goods to one Bogus Litmus, who had the stones re-cut and sold them as counterfeit menhirs. Now you have to find the ship in question, and then you'll have all the evidence you need.

Unfortunately Caius has forgotten the name of the ship, but he knows friends of Litmus, both Egyptian and Roman, who are sure to know more. Where can you find them? Caius says they often mention the baths, where they go regularly. One final detail which may help you: they usually wear red clothes.

● It can't be said you know very much more. It's time you ventured out into Rome with these slight clues. Go to **215**.

230

The steam in the sudatorium* has not entirely hidden a Roman in a bright red towel from your sight. He is sitting on a stone bench at the back of the room. If you want to speak to him you'll have to make your way through the hot vapour.

● You don't miss much, but have you missed anything in this mist? Think before going to **242**.
● Alternatively, go and get demystified in another part of the baths.

* Steam room.

231

The groans are coming from a massage table on which a Roman is being energetically pummelled. A man wrapped in a red towel is lying at the back of the room.
● Go over to him at **221**.

232

The Roman was not alone, and now you'll have to explain yourself to his faithful servant, who advances on you and grabs you. He's a real giant: *he has a Fighting Fitness score of 18*!

● The servant has got the better of you. Go to **212**.
● If you took any magic potion before entering the baths, a mere flick of the finger will see him off. Go to **255**.

233

'Just as you like, but these are the baths, not a public park.'
● You reclaim all your clothes and your equipment (minus your 10 sestertii) and you leave.

234

An old man comes towards you, stops, and looks you up and down.

'Welcome to the temple of Jupiter. And since when has Jupiter been of any interest to Gauls?'

'Well, to tell you the truth, I'm looking for a Roman friend who might be here.'

Having listened to your explanation, the priest shakes his head rather doubtfully. 'The gods may perhaps be able to help you, through the intermediary of my humble self.'

- Perhaps an offering to Jupiter . . . Go to **283**.
- This is the moment to use all your powers of persuasion and speak movingly of a son racing to his father's aid. Go to **305**.

235

No, there's nothing to cry about . . . you're just perspiring freely. You're much too hot in your ordinary clothes. Put on something lighter. You can come back for your things later.

- Go to another part of the baths.

236

Someone must be taking quite a beating over on your right. There's no mistaking the groans coming from inside the room.

- It's none of your business. You go on your way.
- Curiosity gets the better of you. You go to **238**.

237

The Roman can hardly believe his eyes.

'1000 sestertii!'

He puts out an eager hand. (*Deduct the 1000 sestertii from your fortune.*)

'The ship you're looking for is an Egyptian vessel, with a name containing at least one hieroglyphic representing a bird.'

- Useful information! You must take advantage of it at once. Go to **250**.
- Any sestertii left to hand out? Go to **217**.

238

You cast a cautious eye around you. This is no time to hang about, not while things are going so well.

- You take another look, at **231**.
- You decide to act. In two strides you have crossed the room and find yourself at **247**.

239

BIFF! You have just landed heavily on the ground . . . and *your Fighting Fitness score will be 2 points less all the time you are inside the baths.*

- Get up, quick, and continue your enquiries at **252** or **256**.

240

Phew! It's hot in here! You can hardly breathe. Continue on your way.

241

'You certainly leave no stone unturned, Gaul! You've just named my private galley which is about to set off for Egypt.'

- Go to **311**.

You go over to the Roman in the red towel.
● If you're wearing your clothes, go straight to **235**.
● Why not strike up a conversation at **217**?
● This Roman looks puny. Try a bit of muscular interrogation at **264**.

243

Might is right in Rome! You soon realise that the soldiers are taking you to the arena. Your old friend Caius Fatuous stands in the main gateway, smiling nastily. He pats you on the back.

'Well, what a surprise! Here's my Gaulish friend back. Come and meet your future companions, a pride of magnificent African lions. They have such good taste . . . they'll like you!'
YOUR ADVENTURE IS OVER.

A man wrapped in a red towel is lying on a stone bench on the other side of the pool, which takes up most of the room.
● You let him sleep, and leave again.
● You need time to cool off. Jump into **218**.

Well done! But do you want to go back to the circus, as a tightrope walker this time? Stepping on the soap, you slide in a very elegant manner.
● Keep going the same way.

You meet one of the bathhouse slaves.
● If you have no clothes or bath towel, go and get decently dressed at **258**.
● Otherwise, continue on your way.

247

CRAAASH! You have just collided violently with the edge of the massage table on which a Roman wrapped in a red towel was lying. The table is made of marble. *Lose 2 Fighting Fitness points all the time you are inside the baths.* You stammer your excuses, but the Roman obviously does not like to be disturbed.
● Leave the baths at **236** (and don't come back; you've done rather a lot of damage).
● Or try to question him. Go to **260**.

248

Deduct a dose of potion from your Adventure Slab.
Holding up the column with one hand, question the Roman at **277**.

'Jupiter doesn't count money,' says the priest, pocketing your 50 sestertii. 'But he is particularly likely to reward generous offerings.'
● Go and see the effects of your generosity at **214**.

On reaching the crossroads, or rather the cross-corridors, you decide:
● To go straight on to **240**, or to turn right and go to **252**.
● To take a little magic potion, as a precaution. You never know . . . go to **216**.

BATHS OLIVUS

251

Enter on your Adventure Slab that you have no clothes or objects (except for the gourd, which you are keeping just in case), and you are 10 sestertii poorer.

'Want a towel? 50 sestertii, and cheap at the price.'
- All right, you'll have a towel. *Enter it on your Adventure Slab and deduct 50 sestertii.* You needn't hang around here any longer.
- 'It's daylight robbery. No thanks!' Go out and calm down.
- 'Give me my clothes before I catch cold.' Go to **233**.

252

Don't forget that time is short.
- Continue on your way.

253

'Look, lads, a Gaul who plays dice!'
A rather solid-looking Roman has just offered you a chair and is inviting you to play dice. He explains:
The object of the game is to get a number as close as possible to 21. Start by putting your sestertii on the table and then throw the dice. Add up all your throws until you have passed 21 or you decide to stop. In the first case, you

have lost, and your opponent pounces on the money on the table. In the second case, it is his turn to play and find out his score. *Throw the dice: 1 = 17, 2 = 18, 3 = 19, 4 = 20, 5 = 21, 6 = your opponent has passed 21. If you score the same or he scores more than you, he wins and takes the money. Otherwise he gives you as much money again as there is on the table.* You can stake the money again, or stop playing. *If you decide to go on, play the dice.*

When you have finished, or if you decide not to play:
- Leave the table and go to play slablets at **263**.
- Go out for a bit of fresh air. It will do you good. Leave the place and carry on walking.

254

You realise, rather late in the day, that you have stepped on a piece of Lux Solis soap. How's your sense of balance? *Take a quick test of Skill, difficulty 3. If your chosen Secondary Aptitude was selling soap, you succeed at once.* Whatever the result, the soap will have gone if you pass through **254** again.
- If you succeed, slide on to **245**.
- If not, you fall at **239**.

255

Well done! Two Romans knocked out in two minutes. You have a nifty way with research work, but have you stopped to think how you're going to ask for information from now on? Try to be a bit more diplomatic in future, and don't come this way again.
- Go to another part of the baths.

256

On one side you see a number of togas hanging on the wall at the entrance to the room.
- Go in, or go on your way.

257

'Stop! This is an identity papyrus check!'
Oh, help! A Roman patrol consisting of a very beefy centurion and two grim-looking legionaries is barring your way.

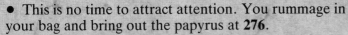

- This is no time to attract attention. You rummage in your bag and bring out the papyrus at **276**.
- A dose of magic potion never did anyone any harm. Drink it at **225**.
- You turn on your heel. Safety lies in flight to **290**.

258

'Welcome to the apodyteria*. Would you like to leave what you're wearing? It'll cost you 10 sestertii.'
- You accept at **251**.
- Unless you would rather ask a question at **292**.
- 'On the contrary, I've come to fetch my own things.' Go to **261**.
- 'Far too expensive!' you grumble, leaving again. Go on your way.

* Changing room

259

You are a pitiful sight, wet through and frozen, sitting in one corner of a pool of cold water. *You definitely lose 1 point of Fighting Fitness*, because you have just caught a nasty cold. You bring the conversation round to the temperature of the water in the pool, which logically leads you to mention the comparative advantages of sea-bathing and bathing in fresh water. That in turn leads to a discussion of the best beaches in Gaul, and, naturally, of Armorica. In your enthusiasm you can't help mentioning the most famous specialities of the region . . .

No, not pancakes, you idiot, menhirs! The Roman, once you have him thinking along these lines, mentions the topic of the day: the traffic in forged menhirs (but he was the one who mentioned it first!). 'As a matter of fact,' he says, lowering his voice, 'they're saying down at the docks there's an Egyptian vessel involved. I don't remember its name, but I do know it included the hieroglyphics for an eye and a bird side by side.'
- Your teeth are chattering so hard they begin to drown out his voice. Go and get warm somewhere else.

260

Strike up a conversation, but first apologise. You haven't made a very good start, so you'll have to use all your powers of persuasion. *Take a test of Charm (difficulty 3)*.
- If you succeed, go to **221**.
- If not, leave again.

261

Enter the recovery of your clothes and other objects on your Adventure Slab.
- You leave.

262

The greedy look in the Roman's eyes as you give him the 500 sestertii (*deduct them from your Adventure Slab*) is very revealing. Obviously you're going to get important information.

'I don't remember the name of the ship, but I'm sure it didn't have a hieroglyphic representing a snake's head. However, there was a picture of a foot in it.'
- This is very useful. Go back to **217**.

263

'Very well, Gaul. Sit there. The rules are simple.'
You start playing with the left-hand slab, showing the shield. You bet whatever sum you choose (not more than 30 sestertii) and then throw the dice. Move forward as many slablets as the sum of your dice shows. If you pass the slablet with the picture of Caesar, you lose your stake; if not, you gain as many sestertii as you staked. If you like you can play again, starting from the slablet where you stopped; you then stake twice the sum you staked first. For instance, say you started by staking 20 sestertii and threw 4. You have won 20 more sestertii. You now have the choice of stopping, starting again with a new stake (not more than 30 sestertii) or going on from where you are, staking 40 sestertii. In the last case, if you throw 11, you lose the whole stake; if you throw 6, you win 40 more sestertii.
- No more slablets; you'd rather play dice at **253**.
- That's enough gambling. The baths aren't far off.

264

What a feeble-looking fellow! If you drank any potion, you almost regret it. Just blowing on this Roman would knock him over. Take a deep breath. *Your opponent has a Fighting Fitness score of 6.*
- Did you win? Go back to **232**.
- Incredible! He beat you. Go to **327**.

265

The old man seems interested in your proposition:
'The priests in our temple are particularly devoted to Jupiter and all he stands for.'
'I may have a book that would interest you. I was in the library of Spurius Virus's house when I found . . .'
The Roman interrupts you.
'Have you brought *Roman Law* by Publicus Prosecutus? Spurius Virus owns the only copy in Rome!'
- Yes, you have! Hand it over at **278**.
- No, you're sorry, you haven't. Go to **214**.

266

It will be nice to be back in Lutetia with 5000 sestertii in your pocket. You go straight to the Consul and tell him to set Doublehelix free.
'Very well,' says the Consul, 'if you can stand bail for him.'

Yes, of course you will.
'How much is it?' you ask anxiously.
'4500 sestertii.'
- Pay up at **284**.

267

Knocking out a patrol with a single blow isn't something all and sundry can do. Can it be thanks to your many visits to that little Armorican village? Anyway, you like doing it just for kicks. Continue on your way.

268

You can't hang around here all day. Gggnnn! Just one more little effort, and you'll manage to get out from under this column. But three seconds later, a terrible noise is heard. PART OF THE TEMPLE ROOF HAS FALLEN IN!!! Avoid meeting any Roman patrols from now on . . .
- Leave the temple at **271**.

269

How can you hope to escape in a city you don't know where you'll easily be spotted? The centurion soon grabs your collar. And to put the lid on it, your gourd sprang a leak while you were running away. It's empty! What a shame to fail so near your goal. YOUR ADVENTURE IS OVER.

270

Well, things certainly are lively in here! You've walked into a positive gambling-den, full of people playing slablets* or dice.
- Want a game of slablets? Go to **263**.
- Want a game of dice? Go to **253**.
- You're in a hurry. You have better things to do than waste your few sestertii. Go back into the street and continue on your way.

* Early form of cards.

271

Lovely architecture. The decoration's not bad either. What a lot of columns and steps! This is a really impressive temple!
● After a final glance at this imposing building, you carry on towards the baths which you can see at the end of the street.
● You must help Doublehelix as soon as possible. Take a short cut to the Senate. Go straight to **299**.
● The building looks worth a visit. You'll find the way in at **234**.
● Why not walk round the outside at **280**?

272

Finally you begin to relax. You fall asleep . . . your slumber is full of pleasant dreams. But did you come all this way to have a rest? What about Doublehelix? He's probably living through a nightmare. Too late now – YOUR ADVENTURE IS OVER.

273

It was inevitable, or at least likely: your reflexes were unfortunate. The masseur was picked up, shaken and thrown into a corner of the room before he had time to say a word. If you hadn't drunk all that potion nothing of the kind would have happened. The customers' first cries of alarm are already heard.
● You've drawn enough attention to yourself already. Leave the baths and go back to consult the plan of Rome.

274

'Halt! Checking identity papyri!'
Oh, help! A Roman patrol consisting of a centurion and four legionaries bars your way.
● This is no time to attract attention. You rummage in your sack for the papyrus at **303**.
● You turn and run for it. Safety lies in flight to **269**.

275

Now is the time to take out your purse. You extract:
● 50 sestertii. Go to **249**.
● 500 sestertii. Go to **294**.

276

Look at your Adventure Slab to see if you have an identity papyri.
● Luckily for you, you do. You show it to the centurion. Go to **287**.
● Er, well . . . the fact is . . . Looking embarrassed, you go to **312**.

277

There! You've taken the Roman's place, and this is the time to question him.
'What can you tell me about the traffic in counterfeit menhirs?'
'Er, well . . . hmm . . . well . . .'
The Roman hesitates, then runs away. You've been swindled! It's easy to see not many people pass this way, and even fewer people are stupid enough to get left supporting a temple roof and frieze. Stand here much longer

and you'll be freezing, too. But how are you going to get out without bringing the house down?
- If you drank any magic potion first, go to **268**.
- If not, go to **286**.

278

The priest looks pleased.

'Thanks to you, Jupiter will be happy. So am I. The fact is, a sailor off an Egyptian ship dropped in here not long ago. He was looking for a temple of Osiris, and we had a little chat.'

'Did he tell you the name of his ship?'

'No, but I do remember one detail. He explained that vessels of his country have names made up of various pictures. There is always a picture of a bird, symbolising the voyage, but never at the beginning of the name.'
- You're really getting somewhere with your enquiries now. The way out of the temple is at **271**.
- Perhaps you should turn on the pathos? Go to **305**.
- Another offering? Go back to **283**.

279

'What? Suspect the Roman Empire? Intolerable!'
Caesar turns to his guards, who surround you before you have time to drink any magic potion.

'Take him away and throw him to the lions!' he orders.
YOUR ADVENTURE IS OVER.

280

You see nothing worth mentioning, except an unfortunate legionary who seems to think he's a column.
- You decide to turn back at **271**.
- Why not question this Roman? Go to **293**.

281

A gleam of satisfaction comes into the Roman's eyes as he pockets the 100 sestertii.

'Now I come to think of it,' he adds in confidential tones, being not at all ungrateful for the money, 'I believe the name of the ship you are looking for contains at least one hieroglyphic in the shape of a foot.'
- Go back to **217**.

282

'As an hors d'oeuvre, here are a few slaps on the back to warm you up.'
- If you drank any magic potion when you entered the baths, go to **273**.
- If not, go to **289**.

283

The old man lifts his eyes to the heavens and exclaims, 'Jupiter, aid these poor mortals if you can!'

'That's right, aid us, do,' you agree.

The priest looks mournful, and adds, 'Jupiter, great god that he is, is particularly fond of offerings wherever they come from.'

Well, his meaning is certainly plain enough. You offer:

● Money, at **275**.
● Or a book, at **265**.
● Or something else, at **214**.

284

Good for you, Justforkix! Doublehelix has been free for five minutes now. But your joy is short-lived. A patrol has chosen this moment to bar your way.

'Are you Justforkix the Gaul?'

'That's me.'

'My men and I have orders to take you to Massilia and put you on board a galley.'

'But that's impossible. I've just paid 4500 sestertii bail,' you protest.

'Orders are orders, specially when they come from

Caesar himself. Anyway, you paid for Doublehelix, not yourself.'

It's just not fair, but there's no point in arguing. Do you have to go right back to the start? Too late for that. You have to admit that you've failed. YOUR ADVENTURE IS OVER.

285

Hello, you're going to have company. Some soldiers are coming your way. Prepare for the worst.

● If you've already damaged an ancient monument, go to **301**.
● If these are the first Roman soldiers you've met in Rome, go to **274**.
● If they're the second patrol you've met, go to **296**.

286

You soon go weak at the knees, and the temple roof caves in. Well, you really did bring the house down! Crushed by the weight of responsibility (and the temple) you face the ruin of your hopes (and the temple). YOUR ADVENTURE IS OVER.

287

'Right, move along, but we'll be keeping an eye on you, Gauls. If we ever find you hanging around here again, watch out! All this counterfeit menhir business . . .'

● You can go on your way.

288

'Counterfeit menhirs?' says the Roman. 'What a funny idea! You really crease me up!'

● There's nothing to be got out of him. Leave.

289

After a few minutes the massage begins to take effect. You are already feeling less tired (*so add 1 point to your Fighting Fitness score*). The masseur also gives you some advice.

'To think you're from Gaul, and you already look poorly. You ought to take things easy instead of dashing around the whole time like the inhabitants of Rome. It's bad for their health, I assure you.'
• You take his advice, and relax at **272**.
• No. You decide to continue your enquiries at once. Leave the massage room.

290

A wild race through the streets starts as you try to escape the soldiers.
• Run to the baths at **222**.

291

The streets of Rome are narrow and cobbled, and it's difficult to walk there with a bag containing 5000 sestertii. *You can get rid of some sestertii to lighten your load. If you keep less than 1000 sestertii, no problem; between*

1000 and 2000 sestertii and you lose 2 Fighting Fitness points; between 2000 and 3000 sestertii and you lose 5 points; with a bag containing over 3000 sestertii, you lose 10 Fighting Fitness points.
• When you have decided how many sestertii to keep, go to **215**.

292

The man is ironing a badly creased toga. What do you ask him?
• Does he know Bogus Litmus? Go to **226** and see what he says.
• Has he recently seen a man with a red towel? He tries to reply at **224**.
• What does he think of the case of the counterfeit menhirs? He tells you at **288**.

293

The poor man doesn't look happy!
'Funny job you've got there.'
'Yes, I used to be the prop and stay of my family, but then they offered me a job as a pillar of the temple. I jumped at it, but I'm fed up now.'
'You are? Why?'
'Well, it's freezing cold, my nose has been tickling for two days, and I can't find anyone to take over for a couple of minutes. Perhaps you . . .'
'What, me? Well, perhaps. I'd be interested to know if you know anything about one Bogus Litmus.'
'Bogus? Of course I know him! Take over here for a moment and you won't regret it.'
• You replace him at **277**.
• It's a trick. Go back to **271**.
• You don't mind replacing him, but a spot of magic potion first wouldn't hurt. Drink some at **248**.

294

'500 sestertii! Jupiter will appreciate your gift at its true worth. He has already inspired me, because I remember that the ship had no eye at the start of its name.'
- Armed with this useful information, you leave the temple at **271**.
- You decide to give a book as well, at **265**.
- You launch into a long speech about your adventures at **305**.

295

Wander along the quayside for a while to get over all the excitement.
- You notice a fishmonger taking down his stall. Go to **336**.
- You go to take a closer look at some crates that strike you as suspicious, at **333**.

296

'There he goes! That's him!'
The soldiers in the patrol make towards you, swords drawn, shields raised. You must face them. *These four tough customers each have a Fighting Fitness score of 17, and their bold centurion has a score of 22. Fight them in any order you choose.*
- If you win the fight, go to **302**.
- If not, go to **243**.

297

'Ave, brave Gaul and skilful charioteer. What do you want?'
'I want to prove that my father Doublehelix is unjustly accused of trafficking in counterfeit menhirs.'
'I've heard of that business. If you can offer me any evidence, I'll hear it. Studius! Studius! Where is that wretched scribe? Ah, there you are! Take your tablets and write down the statement of Justforkix the Gaul.'
- You have waited so long for this. Speak up at **308**.

298

'And here's the proof!'
At your entrance the senator speaking falls silent . . . and then quickly continues.
'I, Bogus Litmus, point the finger' (he is pointing it at you) 'at one of those who are distributing counterfeit menhirs, one of the infamous Gauls!'
There is uproar and shouting. Total confusion! You have just risen as if from Hades in a senators' committee.
'Guards, seize him!'
And you had hoped for a hearing yourself . . . but you've put your head straight into the lion's mouth. YOUR ADVENTURE IS OVER.

299

How can you get inside? You turn to the guard and say firmly:
- 'I've come to see Julius Caesar.' Go to **307**.
- 'I want to go in. Here's 30 sestertii for your trouble.' (*Remember to cross them off your Adventure Slab.*) Go in (perhaps) at **306**.

- 'Out of my way, I'm in a hurry.' Push past the guard and barge in at **325**.
- On reflection, do you have all the information you need for a confrontation with Caesar? There's still time to pursue your enquiries in Rome.

The great Caesar in person! Good manners demand that you observe the usual formalities.

'Ave, Caesar!'
- He replies to you at **297**.

301

The centurion steps forward and announces, 'I, Glutto-nus, centurion of Julius Caesar's bodyguard, hereby arrest Justforkix the Gaul on charges of destroying a building, insulting Jupiter, legitimate proprietor of the said temple, and failing to render assistance to roofing in danger. It's all up, mate, so you must follow me.'
- You're not sure if that follows, but still, you follow him to **243**.
- This won't do! After uttering a defiant 'A Gaul dies but never surrenders', you fling yourself on the Romans. Strike up a Gaulish war song at **312**.

302

Either you're getting stronger as the fighting goes on, or you fell into something when you were a baby!
- Savour your victory at **295**.

303

Look at your Adventure Slab to see if you have an identity papyrus.
- You have a papyrus and you show it to the centurion. Go to **310**.
- 'Hm . . . er . . . well, the fact is . . . ' Look embarrassed and go to **312**.

304

'Ha, ha, ha!' Caesar roars with laughter. 'You must be joking! That vessel was boarded by the coastguards some days ago – it's an Egyptian vessel which had been stolen by a pirate crew. We managed to arrest them all just before the lookout scuttled the ship. These pirates are crazy!'

Your smile is a little fixed.

'Well,' Caesar goes on, 'in other circumstances I'd have sent you straight off to join the pirate captain, a one-eyed fellow with a red beard. I intend to send him to Cleopatra as a present, for her crocodiles. But you've amused me by reminding me of that crew of weirdos. You can have a second chance.'
- Relieved, you thank him and choose another name from the list at **319**.

305

Before such determination, moved by the words of a son wishing to help his father, the Roman priest is touched. To convince him totally, *take a test of Charm (difficulty 3)*.
- If he is convinced, go to **309**.
- If not, calm down at **314**.

306

The Senate is vast, and soon you have to admit that you are lost. Bewildered and rather anxious, you wander around the labyrinth of vestibules and corridors. You

end up facing two doors. Which will you open?
- The door marked CAESAR IMPERATOR? Go to **300**.
- The door marked SENATE? Go in at **298**.

307

The legionary instantly recognises you as the great victor in the chariot race. Caesar has given instructions to let you in if you come to call on him.
- The guard moves aside and shows you a door at **300**.

308

You tell Caesar all you know. His frown deepens, and finally he interrupts you.

'What you say is very serious. First, what would be the nationality of the ships and the origin of the stones?'

If you're not sure, think hard: you have only one chance out of three.
- Egyptian. Go on at **313**.
- Roman. Go on at **279**.
- Greek. Go on at **317**.

309

Such is your eloquence, and so well do you tug the heartstrings, that contemplating all your misfortunes the old man cannot help shaking his head sadly as he says, 'How I wish I could help you. But I'm getting old, and

my memory's not what it was. The last person to mention stones to me was a sailor off an Egyptian vessel anchored in the Tiber. Now, what was the name of his ship?'

He thinks for a moment.

'No, no. Sorry, all I can remember is that it's not the ship with a name ending in an eye or . . . or a ship.'
- You thank him and leave at **271**.
- Perhaps an offering would help his memory? Go to **283**.

310

The centurion has the disappointed look of a huntsman seeing his prey get away.
- Go on through the city.

311

'What you say is very interesting. I'm going to hand you over to my friend Prometheus. He needs an assistant.'

'What's his business?'

'He's in chains. He's looking for someone to try them out. It's a very restful job, as you'll soon see. You'll only have to wear them for ten years.' And we can only add that YOUR ADVENTURE IS OVER.

312

The time has come to stand and fight. You strike up 'Gods Save Armorica', the Gaulish anthem, before engaging in unequal combat. *The patrol has Fighting Fitness points of 20 for each of the four soldiers and 15 for the centurion. Face whichever you like first, but you'll have to beat them all to get out of this. Or you could drink a dose of magic potion if you have any left.*

- You drink the potion at **219**.
- If you win, go to **267**.
- If not, go to **243**.

313

'Do you know the name of the gang leader?'
You reply:
- 'Spurius Virus.' Go to **334**.
- 'Bogus Litmus.' Go to **324**.
- 'Caius Fatuous.' Go to **321**.

314

HM... DON'T YOU HAVE ANYTHING MORE INTERESTING TO TELL ME?

But the old man is beginning to look bored. Cutting short all your questions, he says, 'I'm sure a sailor down at the docks will be able to tell you.'
- Right, off you go to the docks. The way out is at **271**.

315

'Justforkix, although it seems to him you have family connections with a certain Armorican village of barbarians stuffed with magic potion, he thanks you for your aid in an affair which was making him the laughing-stock of certain senators.'

Caesar always talked about himself in the third person in his speeches.

'Of course,' Julius goes on, 'he knew all about the details of the trafficking and the identity of the senator involved in this business.'

'He . . . he's very well informed,' you agree timidly.
'Who is?'
'Er . . . you are!'
'Oh, he is! Now, where was I! Yes! All we needed was evidence. You allowed him to trace the ship and seize the proof necessary for the culprits to be thrown to the lions. They're already on their way. Thanks to you, Justforkix, peaceful trading in the one and only, genuine,

inimitable ROMAN menhirs can now begin again!'
- Feeling very cheerful, armed with tablets authorising the freeing of Doublehelix, you cover the road home in a few days, in the chariot Caesar has placed at your disposal. Go to **338**.

316

The Fifth Legion has inspected all the chariots in the city. Result? Three days of appalling amphora-necks and not a trace of any menhirs, genuine or counterfeit.
- Go to **329**.

317

'To think I nearly believed you! Guard!' And when the centurion steps forward, Caesar says, 'Ravenus, my friend, here's a young Gaul who thought he could make fun of me with impunity. Take him into your legion and teach him how to be a proper Roman.' YOUR ADVENTURE IS OVER.

318

Preceded by their centurion, the legionaries are carrying in a chest.

'Ave, Caesar. We've found this. Open it up, men!'
And to universal amazement, out comes a fine assortment of dried fish.
- Go to **317**.

319

Caesar turns to his faithful servant.

'Studius, bring us the list of ships anchored on the banks of the Tiber. Which should my guard visit?'

This is the crunch. You furtively consult the slab on which you have written down the various clues picked up during your enquiries. A clever bit of deduction should now enable you to point out, unhesitatingly, the name of the ship involved in the counterfeit menhir traffic. Unhesitatingly?

'Well,' roars the exasperated Caesar. 'The ship's name?'

Using the list of ships, go to the paragraph numbered according to your reply. If it's not the right one, you must have failed to pick up certain clues. Perhaps you didn't meet the right people, or failed to use the right words to induce them to tell you what they knew. Now you'll have to begin your adventure again, and be more watchful this time . . . and perhaps more cunning!

320

'This is too much! You're just telling me a lot of tall stories. You Gauls are all liars. Guards! Seize this wretch!'
● You have obviously failed. YOUR ADVENTURE IS OVER.

321

'I know the man is involved in this business, but he's not the real ringleader. Since you seem to be on the right trail, I'll give you a second chance. Go away and don't come back until you are sure of the ringleader's name.'
● Leave the Senate at **299**, and have a good search.

322

Tota Gallia, quae, ut vites, est divisa in partes quinque, a Romanis occupata est . . . Totane? Minime!
● But how did you reach this number? Pure accident? *Scrap the whole thing and start your adventure again.*

323

Are you sure? This might give Caesar something to think about. Go to **311**.

324

'You're accusing a powerful personage of state. That could cost you dear. Do you have any evidence? If so, where can we find it?'
● On a ship. Go to **319**.
● In a house. Go to **335**.
● In a chariot. Go to **316**.

325

The guard is at the bottom of the steps. To cries of 'Down with the intruder' and 'The Senate's under attack', a human tide rolls in. Carried away by it, you find yourself outside amidst the wreckage of your hopes. What a shame to founder like this! YOUR ADVENTURE IS OVER.

326

'You have me worried, Gaul.'
Turning to a centurion, he adds, 'Send men to search that ship.'
Later, the soldiers return. What have they found?
● They report at **318**.

327

What bad luck! Just as you were thumping the Roman, you slip on a piece of soap, and then, trying to catch hold of something, get your hands tangled in a towel before plunging, despite yourself, into a tub of water. YOUR ADVENTURE IS OVER.

328

'Incredible!'
At first Caesar is surprised. Then he frowns, suddenly suspicious. 'Not taking me for a ride with that boat, are you?'
'Oh n-no, I w-wouldn't dream of it,' you stammer in reply.
'I shall send a patrol to search it at once.'
● Wait for the result of the search at **337**.

329

A special chariot is waiting outside, to take you to prison in Lutetia and to join your father. YOUR ADVENTURE IS OVER.

330

'If you have indeed told me the truth, Gaul, I shall owe you a very great deal,' says Caesar. 'I'll send my most trusty centurion, Saintandrus, to take a look at that ship immediately.'
● Go to **337**.

331

Caesar rises and comes over to you. He speaks to you in an undertone, signalling to one of the guards.
● Caesar whispers at **315**.

332

'Queen Cleopatra's own barge! Do you realise what you are suggesting, Gaul?'
● There are some days when you'd do better to keep your big mouth shut. Go to **320**.

333

In the end there's nothing special about the crates, but when you went to look at them you slipped on some little pebbles very different from the cobblestones of the quayside. Odd . . .
● Meanwhile, the merchant you wanted to question has left. You've had enough of the riverside air, which is rather malodorous, and go back into Rome.

334

'Caius Fatuous was right to tell me you'd see each other again some day. How would you like to get together with Fatuous's lion?'
'Um . . . er . . .' you mumble, a cold shiver running down your spine.
'I wish you the best of luck. The pair of you will star in the next show.'
YOUR ADVENTURE IS OVER.

335

The searching takes some time. After three long days of waiting, Caesar reappears.
'We've searched the richest villas of Rome, without success. Well, Justforkix, you wanted to see Doublehelix again. I'll grant you your wish.'
● Go to **329**.

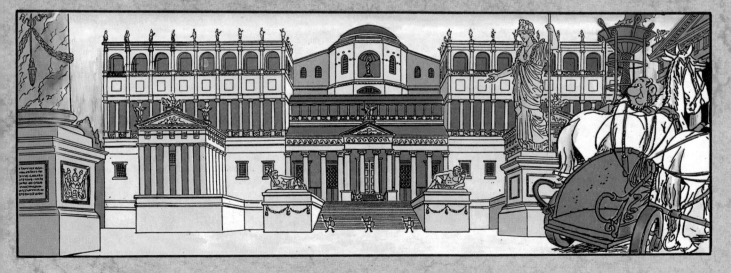

336

'How's business?'

An original opening! We need hardly add that you first bought a herring from him, picked at random from a barrel (*it cost you 5 sestertii*).

'Oh, so-so. With all the Egyptian boats docking now, you'd think there'd be customers. But no, there are very few around in the daytime. Anyone would think they worked at night! Well, I'm off home!'

● Unluckily, the crates you wanted to inspect have been taken on board. You've had enough of the riverside air, which is rather malodorous, so you decide to go back into Rome.

337

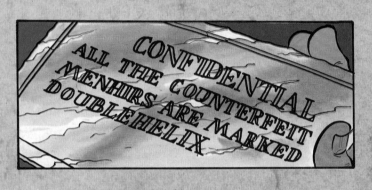

At last a Roman comes to bring Caesar a message. He reads it and then, looking ironic, hands it to you. CLICK! CLICK! A faithful servant has just put you in chains. It can't have been the right reply. YOUR ADVENTURE IS OVER.

338

It's like a dream: your return to Lutetia . . . the freeing of Doublehelix . . . the banquet in the village. Getafix is full of praise for your skill and courage. He even maintains that such qualities are often more use than brute force, although Obelix doesn't agree. Impedimenta has excelled herself in the kitchen, and Vitalstatistix is happy to see his brother again. Together they reminisce about the good old days . . . the fun they had pinching the neighbours' menhirs, for instance. Once again Geriatrix goes into the details of a famous battle fought long ago (no doubt we all know what he is referring to). In short, this is a banquet to end all banquets. All it needs is a little music. What can have become of Cacofonix?

PRINTED IN BELGIUM BY
proost
INTERNATIONAL BOOK PRODUCTION